New Chicana/Chicano Writing

NEW CHICANA/ CHICANO WRITING

2

Charles M. Tatum, Editor

THE UNIVERSITY OF ARIZONA PRESS
Tucson & London

About the Editor

CHARLES M. TATUM is professor of Spanish and head of the Department of Spanish and Portuguese at the University of Arizona, where he also teaches Chicano and Latin American literature. He has published extensively in the areas of Chicano literature, Latin American literature, and Latin American popular culture. He is author of *Chicano Literature*, translated and published in Spanish in 1986. Tatum was also for several years editor of publications of the *Latin American Literary Review*. He is coeditor of the journal *Studies in Latin American Popular Culture*.

Partial funding for this book was provided by the Arizona Commission on the Arts through appropriations from the Arizona State Legislature and grants from the National Endowment for the Arts.

The University of Arizona Press
Copyright © 1992
Arizona Board of Regents
All Rights Reserved

 ⊗ This book is printed on acid-free, archival-quality paper.
Manufactured in the United States of America.

97 96 95 94 93   6 5 4 3 2

New Chicana/Chicano writing
ISSN 1058-2770

Contents

Introduction

Charles M. Tatum

Like the first anthology, *New Chicana/Chicano Writing* 2 offers
a wide variety of narrative and poetic styles, linguistic us-
ages, and themes. The writers included in these pages con-
tinue to reflect Chicana/Chicano literature's dynamism and
change. They serve to demonstrate that this literature is multi-
dimensional and multivocal.

With two exceptions—Joel Huerta and Pat Mora—none of
the writers in this volume appears in the first volume. We are
very pleased by the response to our call for manuscripts and
the fine quality of the writing submitted. Readers will be
familiar with some of the writers appearing in this edition
(e.g., Miguel Méndez, María Herrera-Sobek, Dagoberto Gilb,
and Inés Hernández), while others (e.g., Rita Magdaleno,
Rowena Rivera, Ed Chávez) are relatively unknown, at least
nationally.

Dagoberto Gilb, Ed Chávez, and Rowena Rivera each offer
a finely rendered short narrative work with keen psychological insight. Gilb's character in "Romero's Shirt" responds posi-
tively to the loss of a treasured personal item as he seems
poised to break out of his self-imposed emotional isolation.
Chávez paints with deft strokes several men's ambivalent reactions to their mother's death. Rivera's *santero*, Don Cas-
miro, reminds us of García Márquez's Baltazar, the maker of
fine bird cages. Both are talented artisans who play an important role in their respective rural communities. Moreover, the
role of death gives Rivera's tale a magically real quality common to the Colombian's narrative. All three stories demonstrate a skilled and controlled use of understatement.

Miguel Méndez's and Margarita Tavera Rivera's narrative
pieces are experimental, Mendez's because of its interesting

manipulation of structure and multiple linguistic levels, Rivera's owing to its pervasive hallucinatory quality. Readers will be familiar with Méndez's masterful use of oral language in works such as *Peregrinos de Aztlán*. His metafictional piece, "Ledras y latrillos," goes well beyond his earlier work as he skillfully alternates between standard, *pachuco*, and medieval Spanish. His narrator—a character himself—comments on language, character, culture, and the creative process. Rivera's anonymous character evokes the physical and psychological pain of a person slowly succumbing to rabies.

Two of the poets, Inés Hernández and Rita Magdaleno, deal with the frustration of being women and members of a minority group. Hernández's long poem, "Testimonio de memoria," harkens back to the height of the Chicano Movement. She angrily recounts the inferior role to which women were relegated by their Chicano counterparts. Magdaleno's poetry, while accommodating the pain and humiliation of a woman's forced secondary role, provides an alternative: the strength derived from the company of other women surrounded by warm familiar things.

Lest there be any doubt that Chicana/Chicano literature of the 1990s has lost its sharp critical edge, Alex Olvera deals with the cost of succeeding in an Anglo world at the expense of relinquishing deep-rooted values of family life and the comfort one derives from a community of Brown people.

An international vein runs through the poetry of María Herrera-Sobek and Emilia Paredes. The former reflects on ethnic-race relations in England while the latter struggles as an outsider to understand the suffering of a culture not her own. Paredes describes her "Island poems" as wanderings of a venturing heart.

Unlike the first volume, this one contains a personal essay by Pat Mora. "The Dance Within My Heart" represents a wandering that differs from Paredes's. An international traveler herself, Mora chooses to bring to the surface the rich impressions derived from the physical confines of the museum where she can venture through centuries of time and across vast spaces by entering the seemingly hermetic world of the displayed object. In her companion poem, "Pescadote," she seeks to dignify the animal world—again, a world we frequently objectify—by attributing to an ancient fish the wisdom and sagacity of an elder. In his narrative work, Joel Huerta reflects on the dramatic change that occurred in his life when President Lyndon Baines Johnson's Great Society finally arrived in South Texas. As Huerta wryly observes, who could wait for the likes of Private America to come calling. Related to the personal by token of their autobiographical quality are Arlene Mestas's two short works "Mi Madrina" and "How Pancho Was Nearly Late to His Own Funeral." Her view of death, even the passing of two loved ones—her godmother and her father—is tinged with humor along with grief. The two-pronged view reflects a culture's healthy perspective on death not as finality but as a transitory state.

Welcome, reader, to another volume amply displaying the exciting freshness and exuberance of today's Chicana/ Chicano writing.

New Chicana/Chicano Writing

DAGOBERTO GILB

Romero's Shirt

Juan Romero, a man not unlike many in this country, has
had jobs in factories, shops, and stores. He has painted
houses, dug ditches, planted trees, hammered, sawed, bolted,
snaked pipes, picked cotton and chile and pecans, each and
all for wages. Along the way he has married and raised his
children and several years ago he finally arranged it so that
his money might pay for the house he and his family live
in. He is still more than twenty years away from being the
owner. It is a modest house even by El Paso standards. The
building, in an adobe style, is made of stone which is painted
white, though the paint is gradually chipping off or being ab-
sorbed by the rock. It has two bedrooms, a den which is used
as another, a small dining area, a living room, a kitchen, one
bathroom, and a garage which, someday, he plans to turn
into another place to live. Although in a development facing
a paved street and in a neighborhood, it has the appearance
of being more than almost half an acre. At the front door side
is a garden of cactuses—nopal, ocotillo, and agave—and
there are weeds that grow tall with yellow flowers which seed
into thorn-hard burrs. The rest is dirt and rocks of various
sizes, the loose ones of which have been lined up to form a
narrow path out of the graded dirt, a walkway to the front
porch—where, under a tile and tongue-and-groove overhang,
are a wooden chair and a love seat, covered by an old bed-
spread, its frame legless on the red cement slab. Once the
porch looked onto oak trees. Two of them are dried-out
stumps; the other has a limb or two which still can produce

leaves, but with so many amputations, its future is irre-
versible. Romero seldom runs water through a garden hose,
though in the back yard some patchy grass can almost seem
suburban, at least to him, when he does. Near the corner of
his land, in the front next to the sidewalk is a juniper shrub,
his only bright green plant, and that Romero does not want
to yellow and die, so he makes special efforts on its behalf,
washing off dust, keeping its leaves neatly pruned and shaped.

These days Romero calls himself a handyman. He does odd
jobs, which is exactly how he advertises—"no job too small"—
the work in the throwaway paper. He hangs wallpaper and
doors, he paints, lays carpet, does just about anything someone will call and ask him to do. It doesn't earn him much,
and sometimes it's barely enough, but he's his own boss, and
he'd had so many bad jobs over those other years, ones no
more dependable, he's learned that this suits him. At one time
Romero did want more, and he'd believed that he could have
it simply through work, but no matter what he did his children still had to be born at the County Hospital. Even years
later it was there that his oldest son went for a serious medical treatment because Romero couldn't afford the private hos-
pitals. He tried not to worry about how he earned his money.
In Mexico, where his parents were born and he spent much of
his youth, so many things weren't available, and any work
which allowed for food, clothes, and housing was to be hon-
ored—by the standards there, Romero lived well. Except this
wasn't Mexico, and even though there were those who did
even worse here, there were those who did better and had
more, and a young Romero too often felt ashamed by what he
saw as failure. But time passed, and he got older. As he saw
it, he didn't live in poverty, and *here*, he finally came to real-
ize, was where he was, where he and his family were going to
stay. Life in El Paso was much like the land—hard, but one
could make do with what was offered. Just as his parents had,
Romero always thought it was a beautiful place for a home.

Yet people he knew left—to Houston, Dallas, Los Angeles,

San Diego, Denver, Chicago—and came back for holidays
with stories of high wages and acquisition. And more and
more people crossed the river, in rags, taking work, his work,
at any price. Romero constantly had to discipline himself by
remembering the past, how his parents had lived. He had to
teach himself to appreciate what he did have. His car, for
example, he'd kept up since his early twenties. He'd had it
painted three times in that period, and he'd worked on it de-
votedly so that even now it's in as good a condition as almost
any car could be. For his children he tried to offer more—an
assortment of clothes for his daughter, lots of toys for his sons.
He denied his wife nothing, but she was a woman who asked
for little. For himself, it was much less. He owned some work
clothes and T-shirts necessary for his jobs, a set of good-
enough, he thought, shirts he'd had since before the car. He
kept up a nice pair of custom boots, and in a closet hung a
pair of slacks for a wedding or baptism or an important mass.
He owned two jackets, a leather one from Mexico and a
warm nylon one for cold work days. And he owned a wool
plaid shirt, a Pendleton and his favorite piece of clothing,
which he'd bought right after the car and before his marriage
because it really was good-looking besides being functional.
He wore it anywhere and everywhere with confidence that its
quality would always be both in style and appropriate.

* * *

The border was less than two miles below Romero's home,
and he could see, down the dirt street which ran alongside his
property, the desert and mountains in Mexico. The street was
one of the few in the city which hadn't yet been paved. Romero liked it that way, despite the run-off problems when
heavy rains passed by, as they had the day before this day. A
night wind had blown hard behind the rains, and the air was
so clean he could easily see buildings in Juárez. It was sunny,
but a breeze told him to put on his favorite shirt before he
pulled the car up alongside the house and dragged over the

garden hose to wash it, which was something he still enjoyed doing as much as anything else. He was organized, had a special bucket, a special sponge, and he used warm water from the kitchen sink. When he started soaping the car he worried about getting his shirt sleeves wet, and once he was moving around he decided a T-shirt would keep him warm enough. So he took off the wool shirt and draped it, conspicuously, over the juniper near him, at the corner of his property. He thought that if he couldn't help but see it, he couldn't forget it, and forgetting something outside was losing it. He lived near a school, and teenagers passed by all the time, and then also there was a regular foot traffic—many people walked the sidewalk in front of his house, many who had no work.

After the car was washed, Romero went inside and brought out the car wax. Waxing his car was another thing he still liked to do, especially on a weekday like this one when he was by himself, when no one in his family was home. He could work faster, but he took his time, spreading with a damp cloth, waiting, then wiping off the crust with the dry cloth. The exterior done, he went inside the car and waxed the dash, picked up some trash on the floorboard, cleaned out the glove compartment. Then he went for some pliers he kept in a toolbox in the garage, returned, and began to wire up the rear license place which had lost a nut and bolt and was hanging awkwardly. As he did this, he thought of other things he might do when he finished, like prune the juniper. Except his old shears had broken, and he hadn't found another used pair, because he wouldn't buy them new.

An old man walked up to him carrying a garden rake, a hoe, and some shears. He asked Romero if there was some yard work needing to be done. After spring tall weeds grew in many yards, but it seemed a dumb question this time of year, particularly since there was obviously so little to be done ever in Romero's yard. But Romero listened to the old man's suggestion. There were still a few weeds over there, and he could

rake the dirt so it'd be even and level, he could clip that
shrub, and probably there was something in the back if he
were to look. Romero was usually brusque with requests such
as these, but he found the old man unique and likable and he
listened and finally asked how much he would want for all
those tasks. The old man thought as quickly as he spoke and
threw out a number. Ten. Romero repeated the number, ques-
tioningly, and the old man backed up, saying well, eight,
seven. Romero asked if that was for everything. Yes sir, the
old man said, excited that he seemed to catch a customer.
Romero asked if he would cut the juniper for three dollars.
The old man kept his eyes on the evergreen, disappointed for
a second, then thought better of it. Okay, okay, he said, but,
I've been walking all day, you'll give me lunch? The old man
rubbed his striped cotton shirt at his stomach.

Romero liked the old man and agreed to it. He told him
how he should follow the shape which was already there, to
cut it evenly, to take a few inches off all of it just like a hair-
cut. Then Romero went inside, scrambled enough eggs and
chile and cheese for both of them and rolled it all in some
tortillas. He brought out a beer.

The old man was clearly grateful, but since his gratitude
was keeping the work from getting done—he might talk an
hour about his little ranch in Mexico, about his little turkeys
and his pig—Romero excused himself and went inside. The
old man thanked Romero for the food, and, as soon as he was
finished with the beer, went after the work sincerely. With
dull shears—he sharpened them, so to speak, against a rock
wall—the old man snipped garishly, hopping and jumping
around the bush, around and around. It gave Romero such
great pleasure to watch that this was all he did from his front
window.

The work didn't take long, so, as the old man was raking up
the clippings, Romero brought out a five-dollar bill. He felt
that the old man's dancing around that bush, in those baggy

old checkered pants, was more inspiring than religion, and a couple of extra dollars was a cheap price to see old eyes whiten like a boy's.

The old man was so pleased that he invited Romero to that little ranch of his in Mexico where he was sure they could share some aguardiente, or maybe Romero could buy a turkey from him—they were skinny but they could be fattened—but in any case they could enjoy a bottle of tequila together, with some sweet lemons. The happy old man swore he would come back no matter what, for he could do many things for Romero at his beautiful home. He swore he would return, maybe in a week, or two, for surely there was work which needed to be done in the back yard.

Romero wasn't used to feeling so virtuous. He so often was disappointed, so often dwelled on the difficulties of life, that he had become too hard, guarding against compassion and generosity. So much so that he'd even become spare with his words, and even with his family. To the children his wife whispered that this was because he was tired, and, since it wasn't untrue, he accepted it as the explanation too. It spared him that worry, and from having to discuss why he liked working weekends and taking a day off during the week, like this one. But now an old man had made Romero wish his family were here with him so he could give as much, *more*, to them, too, so he could watch their kind of spin-around dances—he'd missed so many—and at this moment Romero swore he would take them all into Juárez that night for dinner. He might even convince them to take a day, maybe two, for a drive to his uncle's house in Chihuahua instead, because he'd promised that so many years ago—so long ago they probably thought about somewhere else by now, like San Diego, or Los Angeles. Then he'd take them there! They'd go for a week, spend whatever it took. No expense could be so great, and if happiness was as easy as some tacos and a five-dollar bill, then how stupid it had been of him not to have offered it all this time.

Romero felt so good, felt such relief, he napped on the couch. When he woke up he remembered his shirt immediately, that it was already gone before the old man had even arrived—he remembered they'd walked around the juniper before it was cut. Nevertheless, the possibility that the old man took it wouldn't leave Romero's mind. Since he'd never believed in letting down, giving into someone like that old man, the whole experience became suspect. Maybe it was part of some ruse which ended with the old man taking his shirt, some food, money. This was how Romero thought. Though he held a hope that he'd left it somewhere else, that it was a lapse of memory on his part—he went outside, inside, looked everywhere twice, then one more time after that—his cynicism had flowered, colorful and bitter.

* * *

Understand that it was his favorite shirt, that he'd never thought of replacing it and that its loss was all Romero could keep his mind on, though he knew very well it wasn't a son, or a daughter, or a wife, or a mother or father, not a disaster of any kind. It was a simple shirt, in the true value of things not very much of a loss. But understand also that Romero was a good man who tried to do what was right and who would harm no one willfully. Understand that Romero was a man who had taught himself not to care, not to want, not to desire for so long that he'd lost many words, avoided many people, kept to himself, alone, almost always, even when his wife gave him his meals. Understand that it was his favorite shirt and though no more than that, for him it was no less. Then understand how he felt like a fool paying that old man who, he considered, might even have taken it, like a fool for feeling so friendly and generous, happy, when the shirt was already gone, like a fool for having all those and these thoughts for the love of a wool shirt, like a fool for not being able to stop thinking them all but especially the one reminding him that this was what he had always believed in, that loss was what he was most prepared for. And so then you might understand why he began to stare out the window of his home, waiting for someone to walk by absently with it on, for the thief to pass by, carelessly. He kept a watch out the window as each of his children came in, then his wife. He told them only what had happened and, as always, they left him alone. He stared out that window onto the dirt street, past the ocotillos and nopales and agaves, the junipers and oaks and mulberries in front of other homes of brick or stone, painted or not, past them to the buildings in Juárez, and he watched the horizon darken and the sky light up with a moon and stars, and the land spread with shimmering lights, so bright in the dark blot of night. He heard dogs barking until another might bark farther away, and then another, back and forth like that, the small rectangles and squares of their fences plotted out distinctly in his mind's eye as his lids closed. Then he heard a gust of wind bend around his house, and then came the train, the metal rhythm getting closer until it was as close as it could be, the steel pounding the earth like a beating heart, until it diminished and then faded away and then left the air to silence, to its quiet and dark, so still it was like death, or rest, sleep, until he could hear a grackle, and then another gust of wind, and then finally a car.

He looked in on his daughter still so young, so beautiful, becoming a woman who would leave that bed for another, his sons still boys when they were asleep, who dreamed like men when they were awake, and his wife, still young in his eyes in the morning shadows of their bed.

Romero went outside. The juniper had been cut just as he'd wanted it. He got cold and came back in and went to the bed and blankets his wife kept so clean, so neatly arranged as she slept under them without him, and he lay down beside her.

INÉS HERNÁNDEZ

TESTIMONIO DE MEMORIA

For all the mujeres de movimiento que saben de estas cosas

Cuando andaba en la calle
de Malinche disque
puta callejera
tú sabes
traicionera
        pues
        miraba muchas cosas
               como pájaro andaba
               de rama en rama
               contemplando
               y fijándome
               nomás
Sometimes por ejemplo
nomás de cabrona
llegaba tarde a las pachangas
un "sneak attack" so to speak
un reconaissance exercise
        pa' ver, you know
        y pa' star también
        con la bola
        la indiada
        pa' bailar unos cuantos
        y cuando me entraban
        las ganas

pa' cantar unos cuantos
también
I'd step onto the stage you know
sabes cómo
I'd go up there with the guys
to check it out from up there
Siempre me invitation el Devón
y el Chacón
y entre todos
hasta con los escorpiones
lanzaba también mi voz
y miraba el war dance desde arriba

"Yo les digo a mis amigos
los que les gusta tomar
que nunca se den al vicio
que los pueda dominar
que en este mundo tirano
hay que sabernos tantear"

Híjole, el tanteo
That's why I'd get there late
you know
to avoid all the pre-figuring-out
"who were you going to get it on with
later that night" witty repartee
the ritual of the chase
where anything and everything was/is
always possible
you know

Friendship, trust, sisterhood
brotherhood tú sabes
carnalismo

were concepts remembered
with each head throb
of the morning after cruda
the waking up in strange rooms
where the ceiling and the wallpaper
told you you hadn't been there before
looking at the figure smiling at you
from the entrance to the room
or waking up with someone wrapped
around you
who had finally given up struggling
to take off your dress
that you had on over your body suit
that you had on over your hose
Some people could care less
if you're conscious or not
you know

Anyway, por eso
I got into going late
walking into the set where no one
even knew I had a role
They'd get thrown off a bit
los hombres y las mujeres
'cause everyone had más o menos
made up their minds
who they could get that night
but the new element enters
me
or someone else
and the readjustments take place
sometimes abruptly
sometimes with barely perceptible

cautious subtlety
maneuvering
covering all your bets
sabes cómo
and I, for one,
I'd dance
las polkas en especial

"Camarón que se duerme
se lo lleva la corriente
y lo mismo pasa
entre la gente"

like I said
I'd check it out
and show up for support
porque you know
these were always movimiento
get-togethers
fundraisers
     for the partido
     the campesinos
     the barrio
     the pintos
     the political prisoners
     the gente de Centro América
     the artistas
     the mujeres
     the niños
     the ancianos
     the alternative newspapers
     the alternative schools
     the support committees
         of all the causes

that made/make up
LA CAUSA

So we'd dance

and smoke our mota
and drink our cheves
and be cool
and sing
"*Mira, la vida*
Vida pues que es fruta
de la tierra, guerra
Guerra contra el capitalista
que continúa la conquista
de la gran gente del sol"

I guess in some ways we felt
we needed the abandon, the release
I mean the world, the universe
was/is in pain
was/is dying
so what did it matter
who you spent the night with
like the song says
"*Si me toca morir en los files*
pues pa' qué de fijarme en la vida
mis haberes yo siempre los gasto
con alguno de mis consentidos"

I mean try 'em all, why not?
And if you told a sister that someone
satisfied you, pues,
she'd want some, too,
and the guys you thought were your bro's
asked you if they could mess around with you
and the husbands or boyfriends of your

good friends wanted some, too,
and you saw the different levels of reality
happening all at once at those times

and so you started getting there late
to be with comunidad
but you snuck out de repente
didn't tell a soul
just found the door
found your car
found your way home

because if you didn't
sometimes de puro sentimiento
you'd let go
and drink anything and everything
in sight
and end up crying later
or slapping some mother-fucking
spineless quivering-jaw woman hater
silly
or running through the barrio
with no nothing
no purse that you left behind
no car that you left behind
no friend that you left behind
because she wanted to set you up
with some slime
so she could get to the other slime
and be with him

I remember those days
like they were apenas
a puras penas
los recuerdo

I also remember the early advice
of a true compañera
today and even then an internationalist
quien nos decía
"If you want the men to respect your word
don't go to bed with them"
Simple
and she didn't
and they did
When she spoke
they were reverent in their attention
when we spoke
they let the moment pass and continued
as if nothing had been said,
Remember?

Until we called them on it
Until, por ejemplo,
the MECHA women at Yale
went on strike

and refused to go out with the men
until they won seats on the executive board
The women started dating other guys
whites, blacks, yellows, reds, anyone
but Chicanos
and the men first tried to drag them out
of bars and beat them back into submission
But then,
they got into it, too,
the men,
and like Lorna Dee said long ago,
they changed their tune to
"C'mon, Malinche, gimme some more"

Which is where I came in
'Cause I was one of the women organizers
who walked those paths
with my sisters
with my brothers
with my sons

and I'm still called names
and I still check things out
and I still show up
     pa' ver cómo están las cosas
     pa' ver si la gente ha aprendido
     pa' ver si el amor ha durado
     o si ha sido vencido
          por los celos
          el egoísmo
          la competición
          los sospechos
          la confusión

Y también aparezco
pa' convivir
pa'star con la raza
la chicanada
pero ahora no fumo la mota
y casi no tomo
Prefiero la claridad
y estar centrada
y no me importa que me digan
traicionera

si no conformo
eso *es*
no *estoy* conforme
así que cómo me puedo conformar?
no importa ni que me digan puta
porque *yo* me doy mi valor como mujer

nadie más
Que me digan Malinche
eso sí
Que me lo digan todo lo que quieran
Es un nombre que yo llevo con honor

y doy gracias que mi lengua es mía
y es libre
y grita
y llora
y canta
y demanda
y reclama
   por la justicia verdadera
   y por la justiciera paz

ED CHÁVEZ

Polar Bears in the Mounted Cavalry

"Just like Elvis Presley, no, Amie?" Esquipula rubbed his hands in the February breeze.

"How's that, Skip?" Amado looked up from the Bic priming his meerschaum.

"The horse." Esquipula gave a light proprietarial pat to the fender of the hearse. "Elvis had a white one at his funeral, too. And a bunch more to carry the criers in."

"Mourners." Amado mechanically corrected his older half-brother. Amado was always careful to introduce him with that distinction. *Half*-brother.

Even though Esquipula was older by seven years, he always looked up to Amado. Amado was the one their mother placed all her hopes in, and Esquipula idolized this college graduate. The first one in the family. All that work he did to pay for Amado's tuition was worth it because Amado had a degree now. In Economics. Any reproof from Amado was accepted because Amado was always right. He was special.

"Mourners mourners mourners . . ." Esquipula repeated as if drilling for a test. He breathed into his cupped palms to relieve the nip. "Hijo, but it's cold, man! I shoulda wore a jacket."

"Coat. You've already got a jacket on. You wear a coat over a suit. And what are you doing, wearing a *green* suit to a funeral?"

"It's the only one I got." Esquipula stamped his feet lightly. His brown canvas shoes were simply not enough for the wintry overcast.

"Yeah, but it's a *leisure* suit, Skip. Come on! Those went out years ago." Amado sucked in two successive clouds from his luxurious meerschaum. A gift, actually, from Esquipula this past Christmas. Amado had only to express a wish and Esquipula did all he could to materialize it. That's how it had always been.

"I don't know about suits, Amie. I never wear them except when I have to. This one, it's practically new." Amado looked away and sulked, still pulling on his imported pipe.

One day, he promised himself, he'd leave Esquipula, just like that, without notice. He'd do it now, only he needed the allowance. But one day, when the right job came along, with the right pay, he'd just walk away without ever looking back.

"Shouldn't the others be here, Amie?"

"Hell, I don't know where they went. Probably behind some monument taking a leak. They make these funerals way too long. All that singing and eulogizing. I hope when the priest finally comes he has enough sense just to bless her right away so we can bury her and go home."

Esquipula blinked back the tears. It confused him when Amado spoke of their mother that way. Esquipula's stepmother, actually. His natural mother died when he was three, and when his father remarried a few years later, Amado was born. Her darling Amado. Now she was gone, too. But, stepmother or no, she was the only mother he knew. It wasn't right, Amado talking about her like that. He didn't even show up for the rosary last night.

"Hey, did you know my real mother's buried in this same seminary . . ."

"Cemetery."

". . . only I couldn't tell you where. I'd ask Papá, but he's so sick with that Old Timer's Disease and he can't remember nothing."

Amado snorted in exasperation.

"Mounted Cavalry. That's where Jesus died, no?"

"CALvary!" Amado knocked the dottle loose with a loud thunk on the fender.

"Cavalry, cavalry, cavalry. . . . I feel so sorry for him, sometimes. Jesus, I mean. I know you're not supposed to feel sorry for God, but for Jesus I do. Getting nailed like that."

Amado studiously scraped the bowl with his penknife. Esquipula, still hopping from foot to foot, fondled his boutonniere. The white carnation was pierced with a straight pin through his lapel, a desecration that shocked Esquipula. Still, he was so proud. Never had he been so lavishly adorned.

"When I get home I'm going to put my corsage in the icebox . . ."

"Refrigerator! And that's not a corsage! Corsages are for women."

". . . and I'm going to keep it for as long as it lasts. Then I'll close it in a book. The Bible. A souvenir from Mama's funeral."

"Well, looka here. They finally decided to show up. Hey! Where you guys been?" Amado closed the knife and dropped it with the pipe into his pocket.

"The director wants us to get ready. The priest is here." Ramón, the eldest brother, strode up the gravel drive leading the other men. "Amie, why don't you and Marty take the front? When the director lifts the front part to help us unload, all the casket does is tilt the weight to the back. Skip and I are the biggest, so we'll take the rear to hold it easier."

"OK by me, Ray. I thought my back was going to pop when we started to climb the steps into the church." Amado was deferential to Ramón, not because he was the eldest brother, but because Ramón would not be manipulated. Potential, like IQs and degrees, never impressed Ramón. Only results.

"Larry, take the right center behind Amie. Max will take the left. Skip, when the director starts pulling the casket out, let's you and me lead it out like we did at the church."

The six brothers lined up in their places. Six brothers. Six pallbearers. Esquipula flicked his boutonniere self-consciously when Ramón glanced at him. Ramón was always the strong one because of his undoting love, and always the kind one without ever yielding to self-destructive exploitation. Esquipula respected him immensely.

"I've never been a polar bear before, Ray."

"Never?!"

The mild mockery made Esquipula smile.

"First time. The only time, I hope. It's sad. Especially like this."

"I know. Listen, Skip. She was very sick, and she did get to live for a long time." Ramón scraped the mud off his shoes on the curb. "Amie getting to you yet?"

"Oh, no!" Esquipula answered quickly. Too quickly. This conversation with Ramón always made him anxious. "He's OK, Ray. Really. And he'll get better once he finds a job."

"Well, whenever he does get to you, let me know." Ramón's skeptical smile always pulled his moustache to one side. "You have to start living your own life, too, some time."

They'd been through all this before. Why Amado wasn't gainfully employed seven years after graduation from college was shameful to Ramón. But Amado's diploma stood in the way. The right job just wasn't there. Ramón argued he, too, would like to wait for a tailor-made job, but he had to pull his own weight and feed his family. Maybe if Amado married he'd see things differently. And then again, maybe not. No, maybe he was too much like his mother, which would make getting married worse for himself and a very bad case for the bride. Having kids and being sick all the time like she was would be no improvement. Amado had not even dated in years. Better. He needs a strong, patient woman.

Just thinking about his stepmother made Ramón shake his head. All those years she spent in her room, alone, locked up and in the dark, not talking to anyone. Except sometimes to Esquipula. He'd come home from work to take care of her, and then their father, too, when he started to get sick. Esquipula took care of him until he got so bad they had to put him in a nursing home. It isn't fair. All those wasted years and lives because of her. Well, she'd soon enough be buried.

"OK, gentlemen, the padre's ready. Let's ease her out." The funeral director pulled at the coffin from the rear of the hearse. "We don't have far to go, but you'll want to watch your step," he added unnecessarily. "Muddy ground. Snow's melting."

He led the pallbearers to a mound covered with artificial turf. Amado slipped once and would have fallen, but the director was there to assist. Amado swore when he saw the tear in the seam of his right cuff. Esquipula had to restrain himself from letting his end go to help Amado.

At the gravesite they slid the casket on the rubber rollers over the three canvas belts.

Amado seethed while the priest finished the rites, first in Spanish and then in English. Esquipula followed the ritual and responded in a clear voice. It was an unthinking response because the turmoil was welling up. She's really gone now. Esquipula felt guilty for not truly feeling grief. Not in the wailing, painful way he expected. He could not explain the relief. Such a physically robust woman and all she did was stay in her room. Giving orders. To him. Because she'd speak to no one else. Not to her husband nor to her very own flesh and blood, Amado. Just to him. And he took good care of her. The only one who did. When the Alzheimer's Disease got to Papá so bad Esquipula finally consented to let him go to the nursing home. Amado was always there but he never helped take care of Papá, and he simply ignored his mother. But he, Esquipula, he always took good care of her.

More than once, in a lucid moment, she pleaded with him to take care of her precious Amado, and he blindly promised he would. "Amie's special, Skip. He's not like you and your brothers." Esquipula knew all about Amado's brains. "He's delicate, Skip. He's . . . like me. Promise you'll take care of him, Skip." And he promised her, again and again, simply because she asked.

Only now, with this strange feeling of relief, did Esquipula ever wish he had not made her any promise. Amado should get a job. Then get married. So *I* can get married.

The priest presented the crucifix to Ramón. After a pause, Ramón unpinned his boutonniere and placed it on the coffin. Then Martin. Then Lorenzo. Then Maximiliano.

Esquipula so wanted to keep his boutonniere. Not only for its fragile beauty, but because it was his. He had never had a flower of his own. Nor had he ever been asked to be a pall-bearer, nor a padrino, nor even an usher.

Amado sniffled and blew his nose, and to his own surprise, sobbed.

"Come on, Amie, let's leave Mama our corsages." He un-pinned Amado's boutonniere and, together, they placed them on the casket. The funeral director showed them to some steel chairs where they could sit and receive condolences.

"Don't worry about the rip in your pants, Amie. When we get home, I'm going to take you to Goldwater's, and I'll buy us each a new suit."

RITA MAGDALENO

EMBROIDERING: A RESPONSE TO "SOMNAD" BY CARL
LARSSON

A vase of hydrangeas on the table, this room
blue and clear, everything solid
and in its place. Here, two women
sit together, their knees
touching, stroking the beautiful
threads. One is pale green
like a single blade of weed
at the edge of a small pond. Another
strand is the color of deep wood
roses, wild and very sweet.
Also, threads like filaments
of fish tails, gold
and a blue string curled
like a child's ball, color
of sky on early desert mornings.
This afternoon, pale
and warm, the daughter listens
to her mother's breath, soft
and steady like a small animal
full of milk, nearly asleep,
this rhythm of breathing and needles
sliding slowly through the cloth.
They have planned this thing,
a tablecloth to spread out

for guests who will come
to this room, who will sit
and bow their heads to the white
plates of food. And this will become
a cloth to be passed through
generations, needle of the mother,
needle of the daughter crossing
through the cloth over
and over. A choreography
of hands and needles,
and the daughter wonders
how this cloth will sing.

A BENIGN PROCEDURE
For Nana María

This morning you cup your breast,
modestly, gather it soft
and barely round
after seventy years.
I dress your wound, fit
another square of gauze
carefully to that place
we see, the incision
healing well, they say.

Another morning in Miami,
Arizona, the images were clear
and firm—you in the old snapshot,
winter coat buttoned black
and the sharp gray sidewalk,
your daughters' heads pressed

against you, their faces
weaving into your dark breasts.

This morning in your yellow house
on Moreland Street, I clean
your wound, seal the flaw.
It is a small stitched line,
black path
we are beginning
to cross
to one another.

NEAR A BLACK FOREST IN SEPTEMBER

the storm windows groan
a splintered green. As always,
the village women begin to take
in boxes of flushed
geraniums, store them pink
in dark kitchen corners.
Again, they hear
their men pull on
high black boots, speak
of the hunt,
the deer,
the heads already
mounted in their parlors.

Then, the women bolt
their shutters
tight, remembering
the red smell

that always flows
back to the village.
Soon, they will tend
to wounds, feel one begin
from another,
like a new shoot
spindling away
from its own shadow.

IN MESILLA

wet earth
pecan groves
this easy rain

basket of eggs
en la cocina
warm tortillas
smell of green

roasted chiles
clear bottles
de cerveza

sweating gold
as we gleam
in the back room
warm space

easy rain
afternoon
bright gold

in Mesilla.

AFTER READING THE MORNING NEWS
For Missing Children

Two thousand miles away
they found you in a shallow grave,
sugar maple dropping leaves
on your face looking up
to a world of trees,
looking up, plastic hands,
victim I know who you are,
child, my own hand trapped
inside my throat
for years.
Silent.

I think of who you might have been,
of how you may have loved *sopa*
y tortillas, loved sitting
on the front porch with your *tata,*
safe on blue dreamless nights.
Child, what if I had seen you
that night in August, moist
and still warm after the last
monsoon? What if I had seen you
in the old green Buick, your face
like a fragile moon
sinking into the back seat?
I have folded and refolded
this clipping over
and over, the news
of your pain, each gory detail
surfacing on my coffee this morning
out of the *Daily Star* like fish
I once discovered in my aquarium,

dead, a bad thermostat,
their mouths gaping
open.

Chula, hermanita
I will go out now
to rake leaves,
clear a space
on the west side
of my blue house,
this winter wind
pulling off
the last leaves.

MIGUEL MÉNDEZ

Ledras y latrillos

La literatura es vida moldeada en letras sublime o no. Lo mismo entraña la razón en nobles, poéticos conceptos, allá hasta lo más lejano que alcanza a entrever con sus luces el entendimiento, que en un divagar explorativo en el que pudiese confrontar la crudeza de algún cuerpo de barro animado, chorreante de sangre hecho charca de sudor, hediondo a mierda, a patas pútridas, torturado a moquetes y patadas en culo y genitales, apareándose entre convulsiones bufidos y estertores de placer, contrito y santificado; o bien para peor toparlo embargado de un contento irónico ahora encarnado en mandatario prepotente, porque a pesar de ser un abominable asesino, pasa por héroe ante una humanidad borracha de imbecelidad, enmariguanada con vanos intereses; el mismo animal pensante multiplicado hasta el mareo sobre la faz de la tierra, que profiere voces, se mueve verticalmente y repite, repite hasta autosugestionarse y engañar a necios con orejas de títeres, que tiene él una supuesta sociedad con Dios y en concesión la potestad para dictaminar sobre motivos del espíritu y actitudes humanas. Dado el caso por si así le viniera en gana es en potencia el brazo divino que mata a cuchillo con bombardeos, balazos, hambruna provocada, a todo aquél, aquéllos, que niegue o atenten contra el fuero del que le es dable gozar por gracia y consentimiento del Omnipotente. Eso es también literatura, un ente al que le huele mal el aliento con que envuelve las palabras más bonitas y puras que, al cabo conformarán los versos de algún poema, el más ingenioso y bello. Más allá de refractar las actitudes y realidades con que tropieza, cabe en el intento literario de este ser evolucionado que imita al mono en su paso, mostrar además el universo interior que significa la imaginación, capaz de recrear la fantasía en formas múltiples e infinitas.

Entonces ¿quién veda a mi voluntad de nutrirme con letras a torrentes y de incursionar, si es de mi gusto y capricho en la pretensión absurda, audaz, insólita, legítima o bastarda, en el campo magno de las letras, al amparo de la lengua española hija de los cultivos fronterizos ya centenarios, desde el mundo desértico méxicano, contiguo a éste arizonense?

Sépase que entre vastos duneríos, jinete en este diablo de andriago, con un sahuaro a modo de lanza y de armadura esta osadía con la que resguardo mi temple de ataques viperinos, yo os demando a vosotros quienes nos negáis de hecho con el escudo de vuestra indiferencia y malhadado escepticismo a que no estorbéis el afán que me anima a gritar para que cruce yo mis armas literarias en este torneo en que caballeros españoles y latinoamericanos miden su valer y potencialidades. Si así no fuere, os conjuro por el honor del mismo Manco, a que salgáis a mi encuentro, donde os espero en el plan que pluguiere a vuestra industria. Presto yo, apresto mi corcel a la batalla, pues que ya soy dentro de este campo, por razón de peso en dos tamaños suspensos ¿Quién pues me arroja de estos dominios? Que me valen por herencia ¡vive Dios! mas no por hurto.

Oye pues ya vas para una semana con esas malditas fiebres y tú terco a seguir dándote en toda la torre en ocho méndigas horas de trabajo propio para mulas burros elefantes y güeyes a lo rebaño de machos cabríos ahora que es sábado y que pudieras recuperarte en reposo sales con que quieres ir a la feria ¡bah! estamos amolados y agujereados de en medio nombre no estoy tan fregado acabo de mear a toda vejiga y siento un hambre que maúlla como gata ensiamesada entre los callejones de mi intestinaje como que me salen fuerzas para ir a cualquier lugar donde pueda engullirme unos burros de carne con chile o asada de postre unos tamales de elote más una

frijolada refrita con salsa de chile verde quién te pegó mijita
al enfermo lo que pida da la casualidad que en la feria aparte
de juegos mecánicos y gentío que es teatro y circo en acción
pues hay todas esas fritangas que inspiran a mis tripas loca-
mente a estas fiestas chicanas las adoran mis tripitas no debo
de tener cosa seria por aquello de que enfermo que come y
mea el diablo que se lo crea estamos hechos de la misma
pasta también yo te aconsejo y te aconsejo a que veas por tu
seguridad y salud como hermanos en Cristo que somos pinche Fidelito y tú al igual que yo te pasas reprimendas y avi-
sos meramente por el arco del triunfo ultimadamente es día
de asueto vamos nos damos un atraconcito y ya estamos de
vuelta la fiebre qué hombre es una buena aliada chamusca los
malos humores si de paso se lleva a uno que otro cristiano
mal puesto pues ya no es cosa mía como reza la raza hay que
aprender a amar a Dios en tierra de gringos ummjujú uumm
ummjú qué sabrosura de comida a la hogareña así hasta dis-
fruta las calenturas uno ya que antes de irnos vamos a ver
todo esto que nos rodea pos a ver qué notas de particular
entre todo este gentío de gente de la población del pueblo re-
vuelto con la muchedumbre aglomerada en multitudes pues
mira noto que como éste es un barrio un sector con mucha
gente desmejodida en lo económico pues como que corresponde a lo que se clasifica como las meras masas eso de masas
suena medio achingatado y medio velos se les ven las caras
exprimidas los ojos cinco para las doce pasos de engrillados
así serán las chingas arrieras con que se soban el lomo y ya de
que hacen por reírse en inglés se chingó el negocio los pobres
chamacos no se ríen ni chillan pues sí tienes razón el otro día
estuvimos en un supermercado caro y elegante hasta la madre
con gente bien trajeada bonita en otro rumbo precisamente
donde habitan los meros meros que hacen bailar al perro hombres y mujeres sonrientes con dentaduras propias o hechizas
de pocos o montonales de años toda la bola de fuego y lo que
tú quieras no faltaba más a ver pues qué cubres en la pelota
esa que cargas arriba del pescuezo eso de que si estás pobre

eres feo como pedir prestado no pues como que son chinga-
deras muy pa la chingada nomás para chingar a un chingo de
pelados sólo porque no son chingones a mí que no me chin-
guen con chingaderitas que son más argüendes de hijos de la
chingada que razones al chingadazo ya cállate chingado estás
chingando la lengua del tata Cortés la gente pelada hasta
contra el hueso es fea por pobre no se maquilla se aberruga
huele mal no viste a la moda ni siquiera a la medida sufre
hambre se descolora usa ropa garrienta sucia tienen catarro
constipado escupen a colores sonríen enojados se vuelven
contra sí mismos se medio mueren de frío de calor de acha-
ques de tristeza se escarnecen de rabia envidia odio frustra-
ción les llora un ojo les pega jiricua los joden aquí más allá
los chingan los ricos van a las islas Galápagos sin disfraz
como son iguanas dragones lagartijos si todo se trocara al
revés volteado los prepotentes sin ungüentos asustarían a su
papá belcebú la runfla de presumidos parecerían difuntos con
el hocico peludo los ojos idos la piel escamada con roña el
culo cagado suturando sus miasmas en esencias generosas ellas
sin fajas chicheros ropa nueva pinturas vitaminas peinados reposo serían ranas a la deriva aterradoras monstruosas en cambio las muertas de hambre ya embadurnadas con maqui-
llaje pelucas tacones altos bien comidas dientes de fábrica
aromáticas las tetas infladas con silicón desmantecadas con
succionador podada la papada estirado el pellejo como tam-
bor de moreno selvático rasuradas las piernas sobacos verijas
no pos saldrían retratadas en portadas con las nalgas a los
cuatro vientos un moño de cobertura en el osezno sujeto por
un hilo a medio tragar por el fundío que ni lazo de marrano
con un pétalo en cada pezón coqueto pudoroso es un cincho
que ganarían concursos de belleza pregonero algún hombre
corneta con sesos de televisor y un sapo en la garganta que
croa croa croa la simulación del coito la imagen fondillesca
la industria del roqueruelas órale niñitas de alta estirpe artís-
tica ricachoncitas de la crema acá en la pantalla sí sí las nal-
guitas pelonas abiertitas millones y fama ahí vienen agarradi-

tos de la mano con la misma monserga eterna no se la creen
ni ellos mismos ay sí escupen sus babosadas y luego se abra-
zan entre ellos el hombre invisible se cubre de polvo de cal de
vergüenza de escarnio si habla le emparedan las voces si escribe qué risa se limpian con la tinta váyanse a gringuía indios prietotes güeros cuichis lagañosos el pastel es para nuestra familia nomás ah con que se ponen perros eh órale Napo
Nerón mi general teniente Judas úchale úchale échenselos
guau guau guau mojados muertos de hambre devuélvanse a
sus pueblos mugrosos órale migra los riflitos nuevos con teles-
copio con que balas inteligentes si es un jueguito electrónico
venados con huaraches canastas de sombreros pum pum pum
traca traca traca se jodieron venaditos trágatelos río bravucón
así bravo bravo no los queremos aquí los corre la hambruna
de allá pura escoria en habiendo petróleo para que atizar con
ellos cómo que empleos nuestra lana a Suiza a los EE.UU.
para ustedes estos violines tengan tengan pa que se manten-
gan aquí llegamos para ganar dólares y mejorarles la especie
nos invaden las hordas del sur lo del agua al agua hijos de la
Marilú Monreal esto es Aztlán tiempo al tiempo ya verán ah
con que democracia votos a parir las abuelas y que los jotos
también colaboren más votos ya hermano ya vámonos amarra la lengua más valdría que no hubieras comido en una semana te voy a leer la Biblia para que te apacigües agarras
vuelo con un sonsonete y no te aguanta ni el mismo Job en
persona.

Sin literatura una lengua está hueca. Una lengua vacía es
como un ser humano de corazón enfermo, como un árbol de
raíces frágiles que no ahondan. Un pueblo cuyo idioma no
huella su paso en letras será incapaz de preservar su memoria. Al cabo la amnesia cultural borrará de su carácter los
arrestos que sólo un espíritu bien nutrido de historia y even-
tos sublimes, desde sus ancestros hasta la vanguardia de sus
días, podría conjurar. La pérdida de respeto y dignidad a
manos de los integrantes de otra cultura, soberbios por prepotentes, ocultos tras falsos escudos de justicia y religiosidad,

para que la ignominia, cáncer espiritual de la humanidad se perpetúe en la esclavitud de los indefensos, no podría impedirse sin una cultura viva, arraigada a profundidad, en franca proyección hacia el futuro.

Suele el fenómeno literario en darse como un ente que busca aquí y allá algún cerebro a donde allegarse y así desde su interior someterlo a su autoridad para darle de consigna con imperativa crueldad el que le dé vida y nacimiento para manifestarse en escritos y no morir, por obra y gracia de aquellos ojos que a modo de compuertas abren paso a la expansión de sus corrientes. Cuando me extenúo en este quehacer hasta la última letra, me lleno de rabia y doy en pensar que la literatura nos escoge a los ingenuos y más tontos al sabernos persuasibles por débiles; de allí acatamos sus encomiendas, dándonos a escribir, de turbio en turbio, puesto que de claro en claro cambiamos horas de hiel por un pan agridulce. Empresa más graciosa ésta de escribir, por no decir que irónica, sin ser de hecho literatos en lo que en la acepción más justa del término se confiere. Qué otra cosa es la literatura a la humanidad, sino su sombra, puesto que sólo los seres vivos la proyectamos. Los pueblos sin "sombra" viven como muertos. Preferible morir de rabia y de cansancio que consentir en la muerte histórica para los hijos y demás descendencia; al fin que lo que no resulta legible por anodino, bien está como alimento a las ratas y cucarachas . . .

Hermano, ya son las cinco de la mañana y tú despierto. Tenemos que prevenirnos con un buen dasayuno alistar algo de comer para el mediodía y salir en zumba a forjar paredes con materiales pesados; uno tiene que hacer de grúa por trechos de ocho horas. No la amueles hombre, quédate a dormir, te vas a contramatar si andas todo turulato allá sobre los andamios. La verdad no sé si lo que escribes vale la pena, son niñerías o payasadas tuyas, qué va, noches y noches pintando patas de arañas para qué, vamos a ver. Tampoco yo lo sé hermano, de veras que no. A ver, por qué no dormiste unas tres horas siquiera. Es que monté un caballo negro muy brioso que se llama Cronos, le arrimé las espuelas hasta que le sangraron los ijares y le espumeó el hocico en cosa de minutos volamos por sobre las horas de esta noche. No entiendo tanta tontería que riegas, debes de volver a nacer y recibir el bautizo verdadero en mi iglesia, algo me dice que serías un buen predicador. Empezaré con las muchachas del coro. Cállate, ya te entró satanás. De noche hablas con sabiduría como un hombre temeroso de Dios y de día te vuelves malhablado como un diantre y debes de casarte para que no peques con el pensamiento, muchachas del coro, no vaya a ser pues. De noche dialogo con los libros, Fidel, y trato de seducir a las musas para que me concedan gracia o lo que tengan a bien, al fin hembras querrán algo a cambio y pues . . . De día alterno con obreros: albañiles, carpinteros, peones, en fin, que tienen su habla y modo muy propios; sin pensarlo siquiera actúo entre y como ellos porque no me sé diferente, nací minero, crecí campesino en México, aquí al lado de espaldas mojadas he trabajado rudo en labores del campo, pizcando lechuga, algodón, escardando con azadón corto, he sido obrero de la construcción a través de tantos lugares; soy además desde nacido, hasta la muerte y después, escritor por la gracia del Mero Mero y las chamuscadas de pestañas. No dudes tampoco que llegue a ser yo todo un señor profesor universitario. Por lo menos no eres loco violento, por mí puedes ser Neptuno si te viene en gana. No deja de hacérseme raro que en cuanto llegamos a la labor y te revuelves con toda esa plebe endiablada, te vuelves más pachuco y blasfemo que el que más. Bueno y cómo en mi caso no tengo que decir cochinadas y a la chusma no le hace ninguna roncha. Te consideran porque saben que eres aleluya; a los niños, damas y religiosos se les molesta muy rara vez, son de natural pacífico, inofensivos, aunque necios, muy necios casi siempre. Ahora, hermano en Jesús, un buen tarrón de café tamaño súper, una chorizada revuelta con media docena de huevos más los frijoles refritos, todo cuchareado con tortillas y con eso no me duermo, ni

aterrizo desde los andamiajes; hasta podría caminar en el viento lo mismo que lo hago sobre el mar.
De veras que eres simple. Yo manejo ahora, no sea que tú sigas enredado en las tarugadas que escribes y te tumbe el burro prieto que jineteaste anoche. Te gusta la chiva tatemada, hermano, ya se te hace tarde que no me oyes hablar a lo bronco. A esta hora todavía duerme la gente muy agusto. Los que caminan por la calle andan sonámbulos, velos nomás, sólo nosotros tenemos que darnos en toditita la madre en las méndigas matazones de la construcción, qué desgracia tan desgraciada. Bueno, como quien dice hemos llegado a la labor. Ahora vamos a montar demonios en figura de chivos prietos, hermanito, para cruzar estas horas por mitad del meritito infierno. No otra cosa es este sol que nos llega entero. Casi por nada se le ampollan las palabras a uno. Los únicos consuelos para no reventar de impaciencia o de calor, serán las bromas o los albureos al rojo vivo que hacen reír hasta a los de tabla y los chorros de sudor con que nos salva la transpiración de no volvernos estofado. Agárrate fuerte, hermano Fidel y chíngale que es fiesta de indios, acuérdate que el cabrón que se raje es hijo del diablo.

Orale carnales al alba a rivera con todo y chivas simón que subas baboso mi chili en tu pozo no me conteste así pendejo el culo te despellejo cabronesestos dijo el de los canastos está pelón el marrano el que tenga escame que deje la argolla en el chante el bato que camelle acá tiene que ser de ahuacates pinches putos sangarutos este andamio ta falso ay sí lo falsificaría tu chingada madre no te caldeyes ése el bato que se la tira de boss sirol de mandamás es pachuco por eso habla ansina pos será la tía de los beibis pero es más grosero que las patas que lo cargan si telace chillar pa que no te saque el tapón ráyale la jefa de volada carnal cómo que la raye la jefa uh que bartolo tan tapao te bajaron del monte a sombrerazos pos que le digas que chingue a su madre en un bote de cal pa que se pele toda la pinche ruca eh entre más te agaches más

te lo va a ver no es mala vejiga hombre mal inflada nomás
chingo de veces lian ponido la pompa andar pero pos le viene
iguanas que si le agarraran las nalgas dormido le cai bromear
duro pero qué tal en cuanto le llega al Bonifacio se le frunce
ahí mero donde liace remolino el cuero, el Boni es el único
que lo trai a escuadra y a nivel eh con el Boni le da cosa casi
por nada con el Boni le dan ñáñaras en las tripas a cualquier
pelao ¿ya te tioriqué del Boni ése? Simón ya estufas y calen-
tones conlistoria del pinto ese mejor que lo sepas otra vez no
te vaya a salir junto con pegado que no ves que el Boni es la
misma calaca disfrazada de chavito inocentón órale dale
cuerda el Boni es aquel chiquito con el greñero a la afro huá-
chalo es muy prieto con jiricua está espatiado simón lion
manchoneado como tigre flaquito ríe como chamaquito tiene
faiciones finas pero si es un angelito pinto el cabrón solo
quiande tomao peleya como que se le revienen todititas las
burletas y los choteyos y se cobra a lo chino por cualquier
baba de perico con el baboso que esté a la baisa a la mano
pues uh cómo estás menso ése aprende hablar calistre o se
van a rir los batos de ti aquí con la raza vale madre eso de sí
señor pa servirle excelentemente y que el rigor del clima tó-
rrido ¡chale! ése acámbaros si querétaros que los batos te res-
peten tienes que dicir que trais el culo voltiado por tanta pin-
chi lumbre faltaba más a mí enséñame a parir y a criar moco-
sos ya pues notenojes no vayas a miar gallina miagarrates el
chivo pero ya pasotes síguele con lo del Boni ora que si te eno-
jas me lo mojas si te enciscas me lo arriscas si te vas me lo das
si te encelas me lo pelas si te escamas ya sabrás ¡úuursula! si
eres más longo que la manguera del Chicorriatas ni un mén-
digo gato brinca como el pintito ese ora que comuestá tan
reliviano no amaciza los chingadazos y pues por eso es que
carga el fierro y lo sabe usar quiero que lo sepas y pa pior lusa
un día que nos pistiábamos unos buchis en la cantina La Matanza un pendejete le dijo cueroevaca piinnche Pinto brin-
caba como gato montés con cuero de tigrillo, el bato hincha-
pelotas juertototote le mandaba unos chingamadrazos y pos

le daba al aigre ah Pinto jijuepuchi pos no le vacunó alrededor del ombligo con la fila simón el fierro hombre pues pinche
analfabeto no sábanas ni quién capó al apache ya pues suél-
tame firulais al recle me aliviano y miaches lo quel aigre
a Juaréz que nomás le arriscaba el gorro hasta contra los
que me apachurras sin lastimarme los pollitos ya estás aga-
rrando avión bato sarahuato y que sale el bato en chinga talo-
neando quien le taponiara los chorritos de Ketchup al recle se
aprontó con el carnalito, lo levantó de la cama estando el
brother de rol planchando oreja ¡al alba! ése despierta carnal
apañé un agüite pasa la baisa aliviáname de volada pa darle
en la madre a un bato furris pinche güey estaba calotote de
unas seis patas y tres pulgas y quesque karateca arrinconó al
Pinto en un rincón a patadas le quitó lo pinto y lo tinó de rojo
como chile colorado el güey pendejote se engolosinó échenme
cuanto pinche pinto ande suelto por ahi pa sentármelo en lo
más pando de lejos le brincó el karatecas como aigroplano pa
caile de apachurre al tal Boni con un gritote jijuelachingada
reventón de orejas no pos el cueroecebra lo calmó con cuchillo dihojancha ¡cuas cabrón! sangre mierditripas en pun-
garadas a la semana salió del tari quesque defensa propia
como dijo el Cerveza cuando mató a los guajolotes yo le dije
Boni no andes de baboso tioricando como ruca que le metites
las cachas los dedos y que le removías el fierro rompiendo in-
tastinos tagüeno ése diaque pal rial calletano cierro la hui-
chaca u en su defecto saguán se me repegó muy cerquita con
una risita de boca y diojos pero muy muy maliciosa sabes qué
ése es el tercero quemecho al plato al primero lo sambutí en
un río entoavía lo dragan y no luallan y como dijo don Teofi-
lito ni lo hallarán del segundo no te cuento porquera autoridá
pos del último tú ya sábanas la misma gata nomás que tana-
tera oyes hermano me cansa de oir de barrabasadas si aquí la
mayoría no somos gente loca es que si platicas cosa bonita
pues como que duermes a los oyentes y por qué tanta violen-
cia pues en mi iglesia tú Chente dile a éste el porqué tanto
desmadramiento pos carnal la raza se güelve ansina cuando

no tiene ni madres de esperanzas de ser algo más que un mén-
digo esclavo eso de andar uno cansado y sin ánimo toda la
vida no es cualquier cosa cuál respeto uno sí obligado muchos
de éstos son léperos aquí entre la bola con la familia y los
chavos de noche son otra cosa un pinchoncito de gallo y a
roncar diunhilo este jale mata a los débiles si un bato se raja
porque está durazna la chinga pos los otros carnales le dicen
que dio las nachas por eso mejor se amarra un güevo y se da
en la jefa no no tampoco no toos son ansina mira pallá ca-
mela ese bato vivo gorila nunca habla nomás se ríe el viernes
cambia su lana en la cantina junto a toda la plebe y al rayo
se borra pa su cantón naiden le anda conque le apestan las
nalgas porque les puede borrar las faiciones de un santo chingadazo bato al alba aquel flaco que trai parches en la feis es
el Perro los lunes se reporta tarde reventada la cara toda hin-
chada de tanto que se pelea nomás velo le falta la mita diuna
oreja selarrancó otro güey a mordidas ni él sabe cómo se
llama si le presentan a otro cabrón él dice soy el Perro a la
orden dentre los cincuenta y feria quiandamos aquí arriba
hay batos educadones tiablan como apóstoles unos pocos son
gachos y siacen pa pasar el ratón riéndose tú sabes ni les ha-
bles a los bartolos en sus nombres porque te contestan grose-
rías en versos los albureros se agarran en duelos de majaderías
que tienen que rimar tienen que aguantarse aunque se enojen
es un jueguito retegacho pero muy chispa después de alburear
quedan los camitas estirando la pezuña de pura rabia enchila-
dos con ganas de cortarse los cocos pero si alguien senoja y
tira guante conelotro poeta deshocicado pos se corre la voz y
ya naiden juega con él quiebra la regla gritan pa que la voz se
pueda oir zumba el elevador las máquinas de batir cemento
los martillazos de los carpinteros los motores de los montacar-
gas las órdenes de los capateces histéricos cosas que se caen
chorreras de sudor y todavía así la racita con sus bromas peli-
grosas la babosada de los nombres gente simple ¡oye Daniel!
agarra mi chili y juega con él si le gritas a René pos el que te
cogió y se jue y así rueda la pelota Abundio el que te picó

el gerundio Ruperto el que te lo metió y te lo dejó abierto
Chacho las bolas te remacho el Wily te metió el chili Chalío
te pico el fundío Mariano el que te sacó los frijoles con la
mano Mungarro de tus verijas me agarro no para ahí la cosa
no importa qué les digas de buena fe atento te retachan con
una pendeja ¡órale carnal! barbas tienes en el panal épale
compañero barbas tienes en el agujero lo de los nombres y
barbas tienes y con ellos te entretienes no es nada cuando se
tiran con insultos en versos muy pero muy gachos ten cui-
dado parroquiano porque la vida no la venden los fayuqueros
a ver por qué terminaron sacando los fierritos Manuel y el
Chacho ya pa despanzurrarse allí en la cantina de la Matanza
si no es que los regaña Chencho el Mocho el que te picó el
bizcocho por coyones si no pueden seguir con bromas pesadas
como machos pos cállense los hocicos y si no aguantaron comues ley pos peléyense como mariquitas sin calzones se dieron la manuela y se pidieron perdón ahi te voy en reculevex
pa que te des count de cómo estuvo la movida le gritó el Manuel ¡oye Chango! las pelotitas te arremango digo Chacho entonces te las arremacho responde el Manuel me la pelan tú y
don Nacho y te meto más de un cacho aunque no le cuadre al
Tacho le contesta méteme las nalgas con cuidao pa que no
se salgan ah sí me las prestes pacértelas largas entonces el
Chacho se desbocó por de pronto dejó a Manuel colorao colorao casi por nada ansina le arrimó unos versos enrolló la
monda un burro en una hermosa copa y a tu chingada madre
se le hacía agua la boca ora dime por dondiandas si por Sonora o Arandas Manuelito culito de putito Manuel arrebató
con lo primero y ahi te van los versos de Plaza ya no vivo en
la casita donde usté me visitó ora vivo en la covacha que me
da cuando se agacha la madre que lo parió Chachón mama-
rrachón nalgochón culo de putón le arrebiata el Chacho mi
papá era un caballero mi mami una linda dama usté un en-
jendro de perro y su pinche madre una puta callejera no se
vale no se vale lo último no cayó en verso pos no cairía en
verso pero es cierto jijueputa por estas pendencias se quedan

los pobres viejos sin hijos también el pobre tiene derecho a divertirse.

Hemos vuelto de otra jornada más dura y mas infame por aquello de que la resistencia y el ánimo decrecen. El hermano Fidel casi agota sus energías, sin embargo, no se niega a la conversación, le gusta discutir y aunque finge que le asombran ciertos temas él los provoca, en el fondo tiene un agudo sentido del buen humor. El clima que nos envuelve es de una lumbre torturante. Tengo por mi parte un don raro que resulta un tanto complejo; sí, habito varios planos simultáneamente, quizá porque rehuso con rebeldía terminante el acatar los dictados localistas que al tenor del concepto tiempo nos invalidan una dinámica múltiple y nos proyectan a movernos en una dimensión sola, contra la potestad de un espíritu y pensamiento libres y ubicuos. Ahora mismo me ocupan dos arduas tareas diurnas, dada cada cual en muy diverso contexto, amén de la vida familiar en la que es factor también mi presencia. De noche escribe mi mano, mientras yo ajeno a las letras vago entre vivires pretéritos. De ese modo, sin menoscabo a realidades tangibles me transfiero al futuro, sea ya porque es de fuerza o bien me lo demande el capricho. Estoy al borde del colapso a estas alturas. Las energías suelen tener linderos estrechos en contraste a los ilimitados en que se finca la voluntad, más cuando el sueño desaparece como en este lapso ya alargado. En fin que ya volverá la calma liberada de rutinas . . .

Otra vez la burra al trigo. Te has pasado otra noche en vela. Buenos días, señor tecolote, te vas a quedar muerto que no dormido, hombre esto se pasa de la raya. Hermano aleluya sólo he contado con diez semanas para terminar este libro y mandarlo a unos profesores hispanos a un concurso desde una universidad Lejana un concurso literario muy bonito que tiene como nombre y razón: Cosmoletrario. Qué barbaridad, a pesar de que significas un desfile interminable de tonterías y hablas y hablas cosas raras y muy groseras a veces, te compadezco profundamente, algo más que un tornillo traes desconchiflado en la mollera. Pero qué haces, hombre tonto, estás destruyendo lo que escribiste. Lo releí, hermano, estaría bien como un remedo de ensayo primerizo sobre el lenguaje español y su historial acá en estos lares, pero suena más quejumbroso de lo debido. Son trece páginas en que el tema ha derrotado a mi intelecto. Yo, como un simple árbitro obligado a la imparcialidad he dictaminado que estas páginas van a la basura. En eso de dar fórmulas no se escapa ni el narrador y eso como que ya es coqueteo con la demagogia. Nadie podría arreglar al mundo en base a ideas y prédicas, con perdón; mejor está dar imágenes, testimonios más o menos fieles del acontecer humano, de allí que cada cual saque sus conclusiones y que le sirvan de ejemplo y enseñanza. Que si una historia acierta en realidades y en motivos ocultos, servirá de espejo y diversión al que la lea. Será el sereno hermano escribano, pero en toda esta chismografía qué se ganan o te ganas con años de hacer algo tan penoso, sin nada a cambio. Ni modo que me cuentes que ganas satisfacciones, porque siempre terminas resentido contigo y sigues y sigues esclavizado a tus necedades. Tú debieras ser un pastor de mi iglesia, pero primero habría que lavarte la boca con mucho jabón o quemarte esa trompa con la que dices tantas y tan infames palabrotas. Este quehacer, Fidelito, se lleva con pasión y eso es como pasear el alma por entre las llamas; paga con sinsabores y desengaños. La posesión del oro suele superar todo lo deseable, mas no otros valores que doblegan a los mismos siglos. Bueno, literatonto, si estás hablando de cosas de la fe, te creo. Pero, dime cabeza de alcornoque, ganarás algo con esto, lo que sea, durante el tiempo de tu vivir. Ahora verás, sin esfera ni poses de gitano, ahorita mismo te digo verdades que no consienten duda, ni la más minúscula: publicaré más de una decena de libros, ingresaré a las universidades como profesor de rango elevado, se me otorgarán doctorados honorarios y premios en letras de reconocido prestigio, burlaré a los enanos que se nutren de envidias; qué te parece hermano aleluya. Ya se me quemaba el chorizo de oírte semejantes paparruchas.

Antes de que se te abolle el cerebelo hasta el arrastre hazme
caso y . . . pero de qué cuenta, blasfemo, dices de aconteci-
mientos del futuro, así tan campante. Es que, si no soy autén-
tico autor, tengo sí la chispa que le llega de Dios a todo creador: la intuición. ¿Con eso se adivina? Más o menos, en la
creación literaria el concepto terrenal del tiempo no tiene
mayor efecto; el pasado, el presente y el futuro residen en una
misma dimensión, que no obstante el ser fluyente puede dis-
cernirse por efectos de la contemplación y un mucho del re-
flexionar. Hombre altanero, sólo Dios tiene ese poder. Sábete,
teólogo de porra, que Dios no piensa. Cómo puedes afirmar
eso, insensato. El no necesita pensar, El es todo intuición.
Con mirar lo sabe todo; no piensa porque no precisa de
aclarar dudas, le es innecesario deducir. El intuye de con-
stante para estar creando universos y todo lo que va exis-
tiendo. Allá en el cielo puedes ver las huellas de su crear
grandioso en las estrellas, aquí la obra de sus manos en ríos,
montañas y mares. A nosotros nos ha dado una chispita de
gracia; los verdaderos artistas somos diosecitos. Me asustas,
me enfadas, por estar oyéndote se me quemaron las papas.
Bueno, si sabes tanto del futuro, a ver ¿sabes algo de lo que
será de mi vida? ¿Llegaré a ser un médico de cuerpos y almas?
¿un teólogo genial? ¿harán estatuas de mi figura famosísima?
ja ja ja. Explícame, según tú qué será de mi familia, de mí,
esto es para llevarte la corriente, pues no voy a pagar por tus pro-
nósticos, te oigo. Ahí voy. Déjame sacar cuentas, tienes 23
años . . . cinco de casado . . . cuatro hijos . . . siete más 25 ¡ya
está! ¿Quieres mucho a tu mujer, Fidelito? Muchísimo, es mi
bienamada eternamente; la adoro por buena y hermosa, es
cristiana temerosa de Dios, como yo, la dicha de su compañía
se la debo a El. ¿Amas a tus hijos? Con todo el alma como
Nuestro Señor nos ama a nosotros. Pues fíjate en lo que será
de tu vida y la de los tuyos: En 32 años más abandonarás a tu
esposa por arrugada, envejecida, fea y enferma. ¡Cállate loco
mentiroso! Tampoco volverás a ver a tus hijos y nietos. Lo de-
jarás todo por una mujer veinteañera, hermosa y sensual, más

buena para hacer el amor que la misma reina de Saba. ¡Qué disparate! Emigrarán ella y tú a una isla muy lejana. Allá, al cabo de unos años morirás solitario, con los ojos secos vaciados de lágrimas. Cómo puedes insultarme así, no tienes derecho, pídeme perdón por decirme esas babosadas, escritor de pacotilla. No puedo, amigo del alma, hecho está. ¿Por qué lo afirmas con tanto aplomo? Porque lo sé estoy narrando en retrospectiva ¡tonto de capirote! en pleno año de 1991. Sin embargo, Fidel, tú y yo navegamos ahora al través de estas páginas en labores de la industria de la construcción durante este año ficticio de 1953. No comprendo nada de tus locuras, ni quiero que me contagies. Te aprovechas de que no entiendo eso de agriculturas o literatuyas y retrostivas o no sé que loco muerto, para hacerme desatinar. Ah, lo feo me va a pasar a mí, a ti pura cosa bonita. Tiempo al tiempo, hermanito, ya contaré lo del lado trágico en mi vida en una novela autobiográfica en mucha parte, de la que ya voy haciendo apuntes. No me vuelvas a decir ya de esas bromas del diablo. No te diré nada más, ahora vamos encaminándonos a esa construcción. Como somos nuevos con esta compañía constructora, en cuatro días sabemos poco de ese gentío con el que trabajamos y pues hay que conocerlos mejor ¿no te parece? Te gusta la gente majadera en lugar de vivir en santa paz de Dios, del que soy yo un humilde siervo.

Orale batos a ponerle al jale con ganas simon taras a caballo no te vayas a caireles oye cuate yo te gua platicar de la vidurria de estos chavalones de la honda qué sabes tú de eso je je ji ji ji por viejo es que sabe el diablo a poco no con lo de diablo no llega ni al tercer beis qué curioso hablas como en mi tierra oyes estás muy viejo tú para andar en estos trotes con cualquier deshidratada te petateas bah y qué a mí me vienen guangas todas las estuatas aquí la vida es dura reteduras las chingas con este trabajar de animales cualquiera rinde la zalea éstos se divierten haciendo travesuras criminales porque no les queda otra el deporte que sea les vendría caro pos hasta gozan peleándose con esos insultos tan bárbaros chingado

todos los días construyen palacetes y viven en una mierda de
chozas oye perdona tu discurso te veo algo en los ojos tu ex-
presión como si te conociera desde hace mucho tiempo qué
edad tienes viejo la misma que tú sesenta y dos años cumpli-
ditos oyes oyes si yo tengo 23 nací el treinta qué pasó qué pasó
que no te bañas bueno pues cuídate con esta racita te lo dice
un viejo no puedo acordarme de ti viejo noto que eres como
yo medio mil lenguas a veces bronco pachuco pocho y licen-
ciado cuando te peinas sabes lo que pasó la semana pasada
cuando no llegaban todavía nuestro amigo aleluya Fidelito
y tú porque dices "nuestro" amigo es que me cai bien el Fidel
Castillo cómo supiste su apellido lo oí hombre cómo preguntas y me ves pelando los ojos como desconfiadote hablo como
quiero es cierto a como se me venga el asunto o la ocasión
pero no al grado que tú porque estás fogueado en tu quehacer
¿de qué estás hablando viejo qué es lo que sabes tú de mi quehacer y cómo? no me interrumpas y déjame platicar con una
chingada aquí estamos en el desierto pos esos putos que van
limpiando de matorros adelante de nosotros se topeteyan con
güíboras de cascabel todos los días uno desos léperos culo de
tintero nos jondió una víbora allá abajo la agarró el Chicorriatas y la atarantó a medias de un palazo luego la echó
adentro del cajón de la mezcla que sube en el elevador pal
uso de los albañiles bien viva la pinche víbora y enojada
hasta contra donde le salió la iguana al Brígido los batos que
distribuyen el material uno deyos pues así medio encubierta
se la puso en la tabla mezclera al mastodonte ese gabacho al que
le llaman Litterjoe pos que se agacha y pagarrar del batarete
con la cuchara revuelve comues costumbre y que se levanta
un palmo el víborón cabronsón sacándole la lengua no pos
que reculó el baboso y que cae con el ataque prieto luego
luego se la sirvieron al negro Sam éste como siempre hablando riéndose a gritos y manotadas fue a mover la tabla
mezclera porque se lo pidió el Chicorriatas lo voló con que tú
estás más juerte que el supermán pa esto que al gabardino le
estaban abanicando aigre con un sombrero duro cuando le-

vantó la tabla agarrándola de lado a lado con sus brazotes ex-
tralargos se estiró la pinche güíbora y le tiró un beso morde-
lón al tinto quiapenitas se capió y avienta la cosa y sale en
chinga destapado con una guasanga tan fuerte y escandalosa
que parecía griterío de una docena de cabrones aterrorizados
pues que se deja venir el pachuco que la hace de capataz
junto con el ingeniero en jefe el mister Adams como no sabía
de qué se trataba se paró a un ladito de la méndiga sierpen-
tina gracias a que calza botas se salvó porque el animal fúrico
le mordió el puño del pantalón se soltó dando alaridos parecía vieja el Chon del Cid se la barrió de un nivelazo la remató
le hizo torta la cabeza yo creo que tenía viboritas porque se
le siguió retorciendo en medio el Chicorriatas la apergolló de
la cola y bajó por el elevador dizque a tirarla y que en esto
llega la gringuita muy rebonita en su restaurante con ruedas
si pues la camioneta esa a la que le levanta los lados y a
vender comida caliente se ha dicho órale tragones es hora de
la papa pa todos hay como no arrebaten tacos sanwiches burros de carne de frijoles hotdogs y cuanto les pida la tripa se
ríe simpática coqueta trae unos shorts de ésos que se les me-
ten en el fundío y en el hachazo le lleva la suave hasta al más
feo pos qué te cuento mientras son peras o son higos el reca-
bronsisímo del Chicorriatas enredó la víbora bien asegurada
al manubrio del comedero ambulante ya que subían todos los
trabajadores a sus obligaciones se subió la Marlene distrai-
dona a su camioneta provocativa la chavalona haciéndoles
caravanas y otras señas a sus clientes y admiradores pa que
veas tentó blandito en la rueda vio al impulso de bajar con el
pavor cayó sin saber de ella pues ahi va el villano de la pelí-
cula con las patas en la nuca quiotro había de ser si no el
mismo demonio del Chicorriatas le metió un brazo por entre
las piernas con el otro le rodió el pescuezo la arrimó a una
sombra entre todos los obreros le acabalaron cerca de docien-
tos dólares a dos por piocha hipiando y a sollozos los agarró
con una risita y al rato se peló a seguir su negocio el pendejo
del Chicorriatas no pudo con tanta gloria y empezó a regarla

que cuando le metió la mano por entre la blusa le agarró una chichi pelona y quesque también le canalió donde tú ya sabes sacaba risión el sinvergüenza que cuando la levantó ida se mio y soltó una pedorrera como cuando Pancho Villa entró a Torreón echando metralla se desapareció el Chicorriatas sabe pa dónde la cuestión de las víboras no paró ahí los diablos de los tractores echan dos o tres en los carros muy seguido a lora de salida todos andamos asomándonos de lejos por aquello de las termópilas a más de cuatro se les ha ido la tripa cuando oyen sonar los cascabeles debajo de los asientos o a la vista porque me miras tan fijamente así tan pensativo pues qué no te gustó la historia sí . . . haces entretenida la historia . . . alguien . . . no sé quién tengo la idea de que me la platicó con las mismitas palabras y gestos yo diría hace algún tiempecito no sé como si apenas han pasado unos ocho días de todo esto oye viejo no no lo puedo creer a ver cómo te llamas dime tu nombre completito ah jodido me está hablando Simón el Pe- lagallos orita vengo oye Chente cómo se llama el viejo ese sepa la madre empezó ahora lo único que sé es que todos le dicen el viejo el mismo mayordomo preguntó hace ratito "órale batos quién es el güey que trajo a ese pinche ruco pa que se lo lleve de volada pa su chante" ¡chale! se me borra el ruco y no me da la feis desde la baraña quiero preguntarle cuántos perros hay enlorca y pos naranjas dulces deja que lo apañe orita vengo Chatunga voy al excusado ese carnalito no vaya a la crepa el toliro o al esquiusmi como querétaros huache ése por los cuatro laredos tamos levantando paderes ¿se da count? pos la crepa ta enmedio el bato que se mete se jode toda la raza lecha ladrillazo al cuartito lotro día me metí a tirar la masa chale pos que caiban los bombazos en el roof de láminas y en las tablas de los laredos me dio escame diamadre sabes qué mejor calmate un reclito questén aquí los chingones pan- tonces naiden te lavacer chillona porque les dan aigre si los apañan en la movida diotro modelo nel mejor hazte en los chones vale más la life que los tramados y aunque jiedas a gato dijunto te doy pitazo porqueres camarón suave bato al

alba qué no simon taras en mulas no te vayas a caireles comues viernes día de las conchas cuando hace caca el águila
pos vamos a la Matanza a cambiar los cheques y de paso nos
echamos unas heladas hermano ahi que te den un aventón los
camaradas tú sabes que yo no me paro en la Matanza no te
preocupes Fidelito ahi te alcanzo después de la Matanza co-
memos algo en algún lado ya nochecita a dormir oye viejo
vas a la Matanza pues natural con zeta a platicar contigo por
cierto para que sepas quién soy yo y quién eras tú si este viejo
no es el diablo en su figura quién más podría ser órale que nos
sirvan una paridita culo de perro prieto el cabrón que se raje
simón ése sí hombre una paridita es una botellona de cerveza
y a un lao la copita de tequila ah pos yo quiero una parida
con cuates el pachuco sabe su negocio habla bien el inglés
como el Lolo se hace pendejo solo pa llevársela suavena con
la peluza qué pues mibuen qué agüitado se huacha qué pa-
siones agora no dice ni madres usté siempre de buti güiri güiri
alegrón aita de jeta caida ando medio malanco con el sueño
medio espantado la pura pelona verdá es que me trai un ala
desplumada un cansancio tan grande que parecen dos pos ali-
viánese carnal minomás sus ojitos parecen de plástico lu-
neado para pior estas copas me están llegando de ramalazo
veo dobles las cosas y suspendidas en el aire como que todos
andan volando alrededor de mí y al mismo tiempo en una
sola hablantinería a grito pelado pos échese otra parida pa
que se aliviane saben qué carnales voy a echar la platicada
con el viejo se me hace que lo conozco de que te ríes viejo de
tus maldades es un cincho te estaba esperando qué razón me
das del Che tu hermano cómo que Che mi hermano de qué
cuenta sabes lo que no te corresponde oyes viejo no es porque
me bebí unos tragos óyeme quiero que sepas que yo gobierno
todo esto que me rodea y tú como que te me saltas las bardas
haces preguntas que yo no pongo en tu boca ya sé . . . acércate mírame bien a poco no me conoces soy del mero Sinaloa
yo te decía yaqui cimarrón tú me decías el Culi . . . ¿el Culichi? ¡Cruz Ramos! ¿Cruz eres tú? pues qué está pasando aquí

oye si yo soy el que ha vuelto acá para reconstruir un tanto esta atmósfera de los cincuenta es una vocación que me distrae y pues para acordarme de cómo era la raza entonces cómo hablaba qué pensaba cómo vivía todo lo que nos concierne para ser completos para que vayan sabiendo los nuevos del rastro que hemos venido trazando ya ves que todo se borra pronto si nos atenemos al viento para huellar las cosas que no deben olvidarse sí sí ya ya sigues escribiendo ya lo hacías entonces aparte de que te jodes en estas chinguizas que le chupan a uno todos los jugos manejando materiales pesados a ritmo de carreras y guardándose uno de un destripe desde las alturas luego tu plano académico tus estudiantes no'mbre no la chingues administra tus energías y eso Cruz cómo lo has llegado a saber bah los chismes son como los pájaros vuelan y cantan por todas partes además yo ya estoy a un pasito de otra dimensión donde nadie ni los escritores saben nada de nada aparte de especulaciones sin cosa de peso pa que veas Cruz no sé si esto es verdad tengo noches y más noches que no duermo nomás escribo por el tesón de terminar este recorrido literario a tiempo aparte de las friegas arrieras al ras del sol pues también el rigor de la chamba en ese otro nivel que comentaste estoy agotadísimo con una calentura que me tatema hasta los tétanos y un poquito perturbado por estas copas no tú no puedes estar aquí por tu propia voluntad veo visiones no es posible que te oiga estoy desvariando no no escritor de los arenales es al revés volteado soy yo el mero petatero el que desvaría estoy en las últimas boqueadas ahorita mismo estoy en agonía allá en Mazatlán pa que veas pa serte franco si no me escurro aquí en tu cosmos particular ya no habría de piña cuando entré en el delirio más tupido topé con tu bromita ¡adió! mis antiguos compañeros de friegas ¡qué bonito! y me metí entre la bola acarreando ladrillos a todos los reconocí a mí ningún cabrón como llegué de paracaidista sin tu permiso veme aquí con el mismo carcaje de viejo sesenteño pitorreándome de tus letras y de tu creencia de que aquí nomás tus chicharrones truenan ahorita estoy rodiado de mis hijos y mi vieja alla en mi casa pues yo creo que voltié los ojos algo pasó el caso es que soltaron el chillido que le da el patatús a la Venustiana y yo quentro en un delirio jijuelachingada muy rarón como quiando en un bosque diunos arbolones chingonotototes pero secos sin ninguna pinche hoja ni pa hacer un té pos onde jodidos ando y el caballo pues ¡adé! estos vegetalones tienen formas de letras muy pero muy mal hechas mira nomás quién cabrones escribió esto la letra "t" uh como cruces de cementerio ni pa qué toco madera la "B" mayúscula como las nalgas empelotas de las miss encueradas de Miami de Acapulco eres el mismito Cruz Ramos burlesco hasta el copete si no supiera que te estás muriendo te daría unas patadas en el culichi ah y qué me harías a ver si ahorita nomás soy un . . . un qué . . . un ente pendejo el pendejo lo serás tú si es de un sueño qué pues onírico de un escrito literario ficticio ya sé soy un ente espiritutiflaico no cambias Culichi no cambias me fijé que los árboles estaban alineados en surcos me puse a leer supe lo de Fidel el cuero con que se juntó todo el mitote su muerte ¡no! si te digo jalan dos chichis más que dos tractores y un pelo abajeño más que un tren pobre aleluyita de repente ahi ando entre ustedes haciéndote desatinar como tú a Fidel pobre tu familia estará sufriendo mucho poquita pena mucho teatro andan a la greña agarradísimos por unas cuantas vacas flacas que parecen armazones con esquinas y otras chácharras y garraletas que nomás no valen ni las aspirinas pa las rabietas dile al aleluya Fidelito que si se acuerda de los cincuenta dólares que le presté se los cobré un chingo de veces y se iba pal lado de la Biblia me estoy durmiendo cruz se me cierran los ojos me estoy durmiendo eso vale puritita madre yo mestoy muriendo tengo elalma apeninas prendida de un pinche hilito te habrás fijado que a cada ratito salgo en chinga a miar no pos es que creo que ya me pelo y pa no desaparecer sin ningún chiste qué risa me da hazte de cuenta que me estás mirando en las últimas boqueadas orita mismo en este momentito jijuelachingada refundido en un cuarto de mi casa los hijos y la vieja con caras lloronas muy ajodiscados así medios tristones con más ganas de que me pele que de estarme lidiando días y noches afuera pegaditos los amigos y parientes afinando las orejotas que se muera ya qué chingados espera pues qué buen hombre el Culichi al café con piquete le van a salir hongos mientras yo aquí metidote en tus pinches escritos así no más de colero de puro paracaidista qué con permiso ni qué la chingada ja ja ja cómo me gusta el orín de puerco ja ja ja cómo la ves muriéndote y todo Cruz pero no se te quita lo bocón malhablado ah pos ora sí jodimos si así hablo yo y no le he robado nada a nadie ni he matado gente ni envenado a viciosos muy buen hombre que he sido yo por eso me muero contento pobres de algunos quiablan muy retebonito y que si se asustan cuando oyen ay una palabrota pues fíjate que muchos de esos no todos pues son criminales hambriadores robones un resumidero de mierda pinches lambizcones mientras te duermes o me pelo pa siempre pa tu información te diré que al Boni se lo echaron el ochenta en Califas le dieron un balazo en la frente como a los marranos en el rastro el Perro todavía anda por ahi arrastrando el fundío por el lodo un montón de estos quiandan aquí por tus puras pelotas de contador de chingaderitas pos ya arrió con ellos tía chingada no vas a creer quel Chicorriatas se casó con la gabachita que vendía chuchulucos de éstos míralos que bailan como cirqueros con música de la rocola están tullidos más de uno con más riumas que besos les dio su nanita Fernando el Chípili murió sentado en el sofá platicando con su vieja contéstame Fernando viejo desatento háblame desgraciado . . . salgo en zumba porque ya miando miando órale camita lo hago drive pa su cantón ya está lulo que lulo soy su cuate el Boni el buen pintor ése vamos en la ranfla del Liebre aquí está también su camarón el Chivo Reyes oritita llegamos a su chante en un memonto lo traimos porque es bato suave misteriosón carnal a veces lo huachamos hablando solano pensativo al recle canijo pero no gacho nos hace apañar patín charrero órale le damos la baisa pa que camine sinirse diocico Fidelitooo acá ta su cuate medio trancas órale simón póngala

ahi al alba nos vicentiamos ésos estás progresando escriberto
oyes vienes bien servido pero si te estás ardiendo en calenturas tendrás que ver a un matasanos un café caliente con aspirinas por lo pronto hubieras visto Fidelito qué gesto tan her-
moso por la mañana me llegaron los estudiantes al salón de
clases con los ojos brillosos y un gusto muy grande me dijeron
rebozantes de orgullo lo felicitamos maestro a usted que es
tan mexicano qué gloria a don Octavio Paz acaba de ser nom-
brado Premio Nobel de Literatura me abrazaban los chicani-
tos embargados de júbilo felicidades maestro felicidades también entre ellos se congratulaban abrazos apretones de manos
hermano estás malísimo delirando en tanta tontería rara
cosas vanas que se te pegan de esos libros inútiles que lees si
leyeras el libro santo no te pasarían estas cosas Fidelito no te
hagas tontito págale sus cincuenta dólares al Culichi Cruz
Ramos no se los he pagado porque no lo he visto dónde lo
viste como sabes tú que le debo quiero que sepas hermano
para que te des un quemón y no me llames hablador que otro
escritor chingón entre los chingones también Premio Nobel
hombre de tanatres me visitó como quien dice ayer se llama
D. Camilo José Cela muy mi amigo D. Camilo si yo no soy
más que un campesino sonorense ¡hombre! yo soy un campesino gallego tómate dos aspirinas más y duérmete ya hablas
de gentes y cosas que no existen ni pasaron jamás pobre de ti
ya decía yo que te cargas una chifladura que degeneró en un
tuerquerío suelto hermano en Cristo Fidel me despido de ti
que Dios nos perdone tanta soberbia y ti y a mí que tu ánima
goce de paz Dios es magnánimo por un pelito de rana y me
quedaba enredado entre estos pasajes pretéritos nomás por el
viejo ese que anda embarcándose y se le había puesto que hi-
ciera mancuerna con él el Culichi hombre estás rematado si
Cruz Ramos es joven mañana no amaneceremos aquí Fidelito
tú vas a ir a dar a Hawaii a un pueblecito de gente muy callada que se llama Necrópolis ahi vas a estar quietecito sin
quien te joda la paciencia ni libidinosidades que te provoquen
salomonsitis galopante vamos a dar un brinco de 38 años yo

voy a cambiarme por un maestro viejo sin un pelo negro cega-
tón con la fuerza de gravedad obligándolo a caminar viendo
el suelo sí hombre sí lo que tú digas pero ya cállate y duerme
borracho terco adiós hermano qué va qué reteloco quedaste
pero en fin adiós y descansa cierra la trompa a ver si te alivias
de la fiebre de lo otro no se va a poder . . . adiós. . . .

Renuncio a dibujar un final que convierta en circular este
escrito cuyos extremos y desarrollo quieren ser remedo del
sino impredecible, por caótico, de tanta vida que transcurre
sin el retoque que algún tirano imaginador le otorgue por sus
meras ínfulas de omniciente. Sin embargo de ser yo arbitrario
como todo ser pretensioso que se afane en quebrar lo insti-
tuido por obsoleto a cambio de revitalizaciones inciertas que
bien pudieran resultar más contraproducentes que felices, he
forjado este relato pensando como modelo al espectro de un
río de letras y vocablos en crecidas corrientes de jergas, jerin-
gozas, dialectos, voces híbridas y extranjeras en giros lingüís-
ticos remolineantes que ya se suman, ya desertan, de idiomas
de paso evolutivo tornado a revolucionario y por ende meta-
morfósicos en grado sumo. Un río de letras y palabras salidas
de madre a las que no las encauzaría ningún contenimiento.

Ciertamente, son los variadísimos medios de comunicación
altamente efectivos, más el fenómeno demográfico que altera
espacios y tiempo, los factores determinantes para que se
efectúen estos cambios vertiginosos devenidos en caos para
aquellos académicos que han perdido de vista la onomato-
peya de las lenguas, hijas de la terminología más vulgar y
para peor bastarda. Sí, un río de letras al que se agregan di-
námicos hasta la locura arroyos y demás afluentes lingüísti-
cos. No obstante ¿no son acaso cautivadores por contempla-
bles los volúmenes desatados que engrosan los ya rebozantes
de los ríos para arrasarlo todo e imponer otras realidades?
como todo fenómeno que dista un mundo de ser estático, pé-
sele a quien le pese y más aun todavía a quien le pesare.

Así que los grupos exclusivistas, mínimos a cada día más
en relación a la expansión desmesurada de las masas, son por

aparente coincidencia los detentadores del prestigio, el poder
y la riqueza. A las masas, en franco crecimiento, por contraste dueñas y señoras de la miseria, se les ha otorgado por
don natural y gracia misteriosa el raro privilegio que consiste
en desvirtuar los idiomas hasta que perezcan, y de hecho el
conformar otros nuevos con la invención de vocablos, altera-
ción de palabras y estructuras arcaicas, la adquisición de
voces extrañas y las que paren los términos ajenos entre sí en
libre maridaje, amén de otras razones indetectadas. ¿No será
el que los mismos mecanismos del alma colectiva del ser humano, por efectos de algún motivo recóndito devienen por
este fenómeno en una venganza ante un cinismo, mentiras e
injusticias jamás imaginados? Si así fuera, queda constancia
de que el buen decir encauzado por preceptos y sabias reglas
académicas, precisa, para reafirmar la solidez y gloria de una
lengua, el que al hombre pequeño se le respete y dignifique
por ser también su imagen y naturaleza un reflejo del mismo
Creador Omnipotente.

Bricks and Belles Ladders

Literature, be it sublime or nay, is life cast in letters. As reason reflects its essence in noble, poetic concepts, casting the
light of its understanding to give a glimpse into the farthest
reaches, so also in the vagaries of exploration might that
beam be shone on the crude reality of some mud-cast Adam,
bathed in blood, a pool of perspiration, stinking of shit, foul-
footed, bashed, and kicked in the ass and genitals; else writhing in the pleasure of his copulating body, death rattling
amidst his brute-beast snorts; contrite and blessed might he
next appear and then the gleam reveal him in ironic mien the
very incarnation of political power, the vile assassin made
hero for fool-foul humanity, stoned on vain pursuits; it then

illuminates the same thinking animal multiplied to the point of nausea over the face of the earth, with act of speech, vertical movement, and repeating, repeating until it, too, believes its words and can deceive the wooden-eared fools that it enjoys private commerce with God, who did concede it power to dictate on matters which concern the human spirit. And so it comes to pass that a ruler might decide, when acting as divine right arm, to knife, bomb, shoot, or starve in order to force those who stand against him or to deny his power that he was granted by Almighty grace. All that is literature; yea, it is but a being of fancy whose vile breath enwraps his words so glorious and pure that form the lines of blessèd poesy proclaiming wit and beauty. As it reflects all attitude and reality along its path, so the enterprising literature of this same evolutionary being who imitates the gait of the ape, does show the internal universe known as fancy, with the power to fashion fantasy in forms both multiple and infinite.

Who bars my way then should I venture forth, sustained by words that flow to flood? I'll enter by my whim and will into that realm of wild, foolish, weird pretense, be it born of noble line or bastardy; on, on to the highest field of letters, to uphold our Spanish tongue, fair daughter of those centuries of toil on this our borderland betwixt that arid wilderness of Mexico and Arizona's barren waste.

Amid the vast dunes I stand a Knight, close by the very Monster of Andriagus, for lance my bold saguaro, shielded by the armor of my valor against the viperous attacks that would lay low the temple of my spirit. Hear ye who openly deny with shield of cold indifference and wretched incredulity and do not dare to stay this zeal inspiring me full-throated to go forth! Yea, I'll break a literary lance in tourney where the knights of Spain and AmerickAmerica do measure yet equivalence and rights! And if it be denied, I'll conjure by the honor of that same one-armèd knight that ye come forth to meet me, here as I wait your pleasure as it most pleaseth. Ready I stand, and ready my trusty steed, to battle on this field where

I await, justified by great reason, to pull the testimonials of any who offend. Who dares now throw me from my just domain? Mine it is by right and not by robbery, as God doth live! Hey man you've had that darn fever for over a week now and you're still there knocking yourself out eight goddam hours a day in a job for mules donkeys elephants dumb oxes better said running around in a herd like a pack of billy goats it's Saturday you can rest up what's this about going to the fair hell man we're aching all over cut down the middle and put us back ass first I'm not too sick hell I've just pissed a bladderful of talk about being hungry there's a Siamese cat yowling in my intestines I'm strong enough to go find some place to get some burros with carne con chile and say a roast and then corn tamales and refried beans and green chili sauce for dessert just what the doctor ordered you've gotta indulge a sick man . . . what have we here not just ferris wheels and merry-go-rounds but lots of people the theater of the world before man's very eyes ah grub to inspire the tripes to madness there's nothing like the food you get on these Chicano fair days rumble rumble little tripe there can't be much wrong with me as the saying goes so long as a man can piss and shit the devil will have to wait a bit you want to come along too now don't you listen to what I'm saying aren't we brothers in Christ goddam friend Fidel he'll take your advice and stick it where the monkey put the nuts it's our day off man never forget it nothing like a good fever to burn up bad humor if you're feeling miserable so it kills a Christian soul now and then if he's not careful so what doesn't the Good Book say thou shalt love thy God in the land of the Gringos ummmmm just like mother used to make it even makes you enjoy the fever let's not leave yet look let's take a look at the scenery tell me what do you think when you see all this pile-up of people these multitudes of man this humongosity of humanity this superabundance of homo sapiens ah well what I see is we're in the barrio poor folk's part of town where you find the masses I don't like that word masses do you sounds a real put down masses but look at them faces wrung out like a dishrag eyes like two burnt holes in a blanket you'd think their feet were shackled how they walk it's all that fuckin' work they do they wear themselves out all that effort having to laugh in English all the time bad news bad news that's what it is look at their kids they don't laugh they don't even cry you are right the other day remember we were in that supermarket where everything costs a fortune smart as all hell and everybody dressed to kill in a different part of town where the snobbery lives they've got what it takes men and women smiling with their own teeth or some they've bought young ones old ones the whole ball of wax everything you like and all copacetic what are you going on about now up there inside that thing you've got on your neck what's all this about the poor are always ugly it isn't true you know pure bullshit you're thinking man hot air just ideas made up to fuck up the poor fuckers but they don't fuck me up though they tell you all that fuck but you don't have to believe it for fuck's sake oh fuck it you're fucking up old man Cortes's fine fucking language poor folk are ugly right down to the bone because they're poor that's all they don't use make-up they're warty smell bad don't dress fashionable don't even have clothes that fit they're hungry pale ragged dirty runny noses catarrh spit all colors of the rainbow have to smile when they don't want to it turns them against themselves they're always nearly dying of cold or heat or they're sick or sad they insult each other they're so mad jealous full of hate frustration they've got runny eyes they come out in white splotches they're fucked up on earth and they screw 'em in heaven rich folks belong on the Galapagos they don't need any fancy dress they're nothing but a pack of lizards iguanas dragons that's what they are now if everything were changed around top to bottom back to front ass first those rich folk without all that stuff they use ta scare the daylights out of Beelzebub himself they might look powerful now but just look at them then like a mass of goddam corpses with their snouts peeled their eyes sunk in their skin scaly scabby

shit oozing out of their assholes indeed in copious quantities
and the women take off their girdles and their brassieres and
then see what you've got take their new clothes and make-up
and vitamins and hairdos and all the rest away hell they'd be
nothing but a lot of lost frogs hopping around they'd really
scare you horrible but take these poor women and paint them
put a wig on them high heels good food false teeth perfume
blow their boobs up with silicone suck out the lard with one
of those machines lift their chins stretch their wrinkles tight
like a bongo boom boom got a guy from the jungle tapping it
shave their legs under their arms bikini area hell they'd look
good enough for magazine covers too with their buns on view
and a fancy bit up front tied round their ass with a G-string
you can't see must be hidden in the shit like a pig's rope a
petal on each tit very pretty too very modest it's a cinch
they'd win all the beauty contests out there on TV with that
idiot announcer croak croak with a frog in his throat can't
you just see them walking around wiggling like you'd think
they were having it off showing their asses yeah but it's
turned into an industry nowadays all that rock 'n' roll stuff
you've got daughters of the big names doing it now showing
their asses and everything else fame and money they've got it
all wrapped up who's this with them ah you might have
guessed same old story goddamned politicians they don't believe a word they say just spit it out and there they go slapping their backs shaking hands all around and nobody sees
the man in the street covered in dust in dirt in shame in scorn
wall him up if he speaks let him write it's a laugh they'll wipe
their asses on it always the same go to Gringo land dirty Indian get out you lazy bum you'll get your pie in the sky but
the cake now's for us dare to speak up and ah we're getting
above ourselves aren't we set the dogs on them sic'em Napo-
leon Nero General Judas sic'em sic'em woof woof woof goddamned starving wetbacks get back to your own filthy coun-
tries hey look at these new rifles got a telescope even the
bullets are educated just like a toy ready for deer in huara-

ches baskets on their heads poom poom poom tacatacataca-
taca gotcha little deer downriver you go the Rreeeo Grand no
room for them here coming here when there's famine down
there nothing but trash we've got petroleum here now what
do we need people for jobs what jobs why we bank in Swit-
zerland in the U.S. and you guys can stuff it see here we come
to earn the Yankee dollar to improve the stock we're being
overrun by hordes from the south nothing lost the river'll take
them Aztlan shall be ours again oh sons of Marilu Monreal
ah democracy votes votes every man a vote get the grand-
mothers breeding rope in the fags too votes votes that's what
we need shit man the way you go on shut up now if that's
how it affects you you'd have been better not eating for a
week I'm going to read the Bible to calm you down when you
take off Job himself couldn't take it.

Without a literature, a language is hollow and void. An
empty language is a man sick at heart, a tree whose roots will
not penetrate the earth. A people whose language shows no
written trace can never keep hold of its memories. Cultural
amnesia will erase all evidence of rebellion from its character, blurring forever those signs of a spirit nurtured by history
and knowledge of sublime events from the time of the ances-
tors to the present day. Self-respect and dignity will be lost at
the hands of men whose culture is alien and whose pride
comes from the power they wield, while false shields of jus-
tice and religiosity hide their true intent and opprobrium,
humanity's spiritual cancer spreads, enslaving the helpless;
nothing can stand against it without a living culture, deeply
rooted in the past but with its eyes on the future. The literary
phenomenon is a being which searches here and there for a
brain in which to make its home; once settled, it exercises its
authority and makes cruel demands on its victim, who now
bears witness to its being by the written word in which it
lives; it survives by the grace and labor of its host, whose eyes
open the floodgates to the flow of the current. When I dedicate myself fully to this task by the sweat of my brow, I am

filled with fury, thinking how literature chooses only fools, knowing them to be the weakest; we who obey its demands, writing from dusk to dawn, while in daylight hours we trade bitter work for a crust. A delightful job this writing, ironic, one might say, and one doesn't even have to call oneself a man of letters to take on the responsibilities of the term. Literature is humanity's shadow, for only living beings cast a shadow. A people without a shadow live as if dead. Better to die then, angry and worn out, than to condemn those who follow to the death that silence brings; after all, if it turns out to be unreadable, it'll still feed rats and roaches.

It's five o'clock man, haven't you slept? All we need is a good breakfast to fortify ourselves and something for midday and off we go to raise heavy walls, eight hours a day playing the goddam crane, for Chrissake. Don't spoil everything man, sleep a bit, you're going to kill yourself if you go up on the scaffolding all groggy. I don't know if all that stuff you write has any value to it, to me it's all a pile of kid stuff, acting the fool, night after night scribbling on paper, well, we'll see. And do you think I know, man? I know as little as you. Why didn't you sleep for three hours or so at least? Ah, but I was riding a wild black horse called Cronos, I spurred him until his flanks ran red, his mouth foamed, and we flew in minutes over the hours of night. I don't understand all the stuff you talk, you should be born again and baptized in my church, you'd make a good preacher. Right, I'll start on the girls in the choir. Quiet, get thee behind him, Satan! You speak like a God-fearing man at night, but during the daytime you cuss like the devil, you ought to get married so you won't have sinful thoughts, girls in the choir, indeed! out of the question. At night I converse with books, Fidel, I try to seduce the muses to grant me their grace or whatever else they feel like, but no woman gives something for nothing . . . and in the daytime if I'm working with construction men, carpenters, laborers, well, they have their way of talking too; I talk the way they do because I don't feel any different from them, I was born

in a mining camp, I grew up in the country in Mexico, I've
worked picking lettuce and cotton with wetbacks, weeding
with a short hoe, I've worked on construction all over the
place; but I am what I was born to be too, until death and
beyond, I'm a writer by the grace of you know who and as
Lope says, from burning my eyelashes all night long. Don't
worry, one of these days I'll be a real professor at a university
no less. Well, at least you're not dangerous, even if you are
crazy, for all I care you can be Neptune if you like. But it
seems strange to me the minute we get to work and you've
got all those fellows around, you cuss and swear and talk Pachuco like the rest of them. How come I don't have to use bad
language and nobody minds, even though they are a rough
lot. Ah, but you're a Holy Joe; kids, women, and preachers
are different, so they leave them alone—they're peaceful
enough, inoffensive enough, though not too bright, not too
bright at all, usually. Brother in Christ, a good cup of coffee,
super family size, a nice chorizo with half a dozen scrambled
eggs and refried beans served up with tortillas and you won't
find me sleeping or falling off the scaffolding; I could walk on
the wind—or on the water if you prefer that.

You're dumb, you know that. I'll drive, you might still be
back there with the things you write about and fall off the
black donkey you were riding around on. You're not one to
miss a chance either, brother, I know it's getting late, I'll cut
the Pachuco crap. All decent people are fast asleep at this un-
earthly hour. Look, they're all asleep walking in the street, it
takes jerks like us to torture ourselves working on goddam
construction, what a lousy life. To work, to work, as the good
man said. We'll raise the devil with the bricks, lots of devils
like black billy goats, so we can ride them across the goddam
heat of hell at noontime. Hell and nothing less. You get blis-
ters on your hands even if you don't work. All we've got to
get us through the heat and the bother is trading jokes and
insults all day long, at least it makes you laugh, even you,
anyone'd laugh, and you sweat so much it keeps you moist,

otherwise you'd be a roast by quitting time. Hold on, brother
Fidel, we're going to have fun, back out now and you're a
sonofabitch.

Hey there brothers ready up there with those tools get up
on the scaffolding up yours don't answer me like that you
fuckin' sonofabitch baskets up up said the basket man up the
asses of all the chicks hell this is hard work if you can't hack
it stuff it you've got to have balls for this job hey, this scaf-
fold's dangerous dangerous my ass nothing's dangerous your
mother's ass is dangerous you don't have to speak to me like
that hey that guy who's playing foreman the boss so to speak
he's a Pachuco that's why he talks like that I don't care if he's
Santa Claus he doesn't have to come at me with all that foul
language well if you don't like it you don't have to get upset
insult him back tell him you won't take it what d'you mean
insult him jerk insult him call him a sonofabitch hell tell him
to go screw his grandmother I dunno just insult him the more
you let them get away with around here the worse it is for
you the boss isn't a bad guy a bit big headed that's all they've
beaten him up loads of times but he doesn't give a fuck not
really it's all the same to him he likes to joke play tricks it
gets heavy going but when Bonifacio's around you should
see him shut up you should see his asshole tighten when
Bonifacio shows up he's the one makes him behave himself
he's scared to death of Bonifacio who wouldn't be anyone's
belly wobbles when Boni's around did I tell you about Boni
yeah you did you told me all about the guy so I'm telling you
again he's got this skin with white patches see and he's bad
news looks all sweet but believe me man he's death itself so
tell me about him well he's the kid with the frizzy hair so
watch him he's got this blotchy skin see all spotty yeah he's a
lion but he's got spots like a leopard say no kidding he laughs
like a kid he's got nice features like a little cherub but when
he drinks he remembers every insult he's ever had and he
charges you for them cash down worse than the Chinese grocer and any asshole who happens to be close by antes up

what do you mean what do you mean what do I mean antes
up man learn the slang dense this guy they're going to laugh
at you around here you won't get anywhere with yessir no
ma'am I can't stand the heat no sir if you want some respect
round here tell them the sun's burnt your ass from the front
through to the back none of that can't stand the heat shit
don't get that crud all over me where do they dig 'em up nah
you upset me but it's all over keep on telling me about Boni
well you play it cool around him you'll have to learn even if
you've got one longer than El Chicorriatas over there it won't
do you no good around Boni he jumps around like a cat and
since he's so thin and can't hit too hard he has this knife see
and uses it too we were having some beers one day in La Matanza this bar see and this jerk calls out hey look at that guy
with the blotches just like a cow just like a pinto pony Boni
jumped like a wild cat he's thin but he's strong he'll break
your balls soon as think about it well he hit this guy and
since the pinto pony was very light on his feet the other one
struck out at air sonofabitch that Boni he vaccinates the other
guy round the belly button with the sharp one yeah his knife
this guy's illiterate no doubt about it you don't know a goddam thing do you man get off my back Fido I'll catch on
sooner or later then I won't give a damn I mean you can step
on my balls and I won't feel a thing ah you're getting the picture kid see how fast he's picking it up well as I was saying
this guy ran out quick so they could mop up the ketchup and
goes to his brother's place and gets him out of bed there he
was gathering z's wakey wakey I need some help gimme a
handle quick I'm gonna send this guy to the other side and
the brother when he gets up he's all of about six three karate
expert an' all that well he kicks the pinto pony into a corner
and evens up his color nicely yeah Boni comes out red all
over just like a chili well then this guy gets all excited bring
on all the other pintos I'm gonna make 'em sing soprano the
whole goddam lot yeah this karate expert flies like a plane
over to squash Boni and you should have heard him yell when

he lands nearly broke your eardrums ayyyyy not Boni nah not
the pinto he'd been waiting with this big knife ay the mother-
fucker blood spurting all over a week later he was out of jail
through self-defense same as when they caught El Cerveza
killing turkeys he pleaded self-defense too didn't he so I told
him I said Boni don't go telling everybody you put your blade
right in to the hilt fingers and all and moved it round to cut
his tripes up you're right he says to me not a word and he
came real close to me and smiles that way he has his mouth
and eyes smile but its an evil way he looks at you ha this is
the third guy I've killed drowned the first they dragged the
river for a week and didn't find him and they won't either better not mention the second since he was a cop well you know
the third same as before hey brother I get tired of all this sinful talk most of us aren't that crazy here nah but if you come
with that fancy talk you'll bore everyone to death yeah but
why all this violence now in my church you tell him Chente
you tell him why there's so much violence people get that
way when they've nothing better to look forward to than
slaving on always tired and hopeless there should be more to
life than that what respect do we get tell me we've got to yes
sir no sir sure you get some rough lots around here but even
they're different at night with the wife and kids around but
what have they got to live for but a quick fuck rooster style
and snore straight through till morning this work kills you if
you're not strong enough when a guy says he can't go on we
all tell him all us other brothers tell him he's just a fag for
turning his ass he should learn to stick it out and that makes
him work hard so they won't say he's a fag they're all like that
look at that guy over there looks like a gorilla doesn't even
talk just laughs Friday he goes cashes his paycheck in the bar
like all the rest of them and takes off for home nobody tries to
get him mad nobody says two words to him he could take the
smile off your face with one punch see he's smart take that
skinny guy with the band-aids on his face that's Dogface yeah
Monday he comes in late with his face all swollen from fight-

ing look at him he's only got half an ear the other guy bit it off for him he doesn't know his own name nah some other bastard meets him he says I'm Dogface pleased ta meetcha there are fifty or so of us up here on the scaffolds and some have been to school too talk to you as nice as the apostles and there are some real bastards too the type that act like they're laughing all the time you know what I mean don't even talk to them don't even call them by name they'll answer back rhyming they do that filthy rhymes never heard of rhyming contests they sing one at the other and everything has to rhyme and even if they're mad they've got to keep on they get real mad too feel like banging their heads but they stick it out you see anyone who gets mad loses the game and the other filthy mouth wins and everybody passes the word so nobody'll play the game with a guy who broke the rules and you get all of them yelling the hoist humming the cement mixer grinding and carpenters hammering then the motor on the other hoist and the foremen yelling like crazy and things falling down all the time and sweat running off you but still these guys go at it with these games in the middle of it all dangerous games they are like the name game a bit childish it is say one calls out Danny Danny take my chili stick it up your fanny making the name rhyme and always something filthy doesn't matter what you say they come up with some dumb rhyme for it not just names anything hey brother brother he's only got one ball since I jumped on the other dumb rhymes can't hurt but they can get real insulting I'm telling you take my advice be real careful it might end up with knives I've seen it happen say that time with Manuel and Chacho ready to carve each other up in La Matanza bar why well Chencho el Mocho sonofabotcho see they've got me doing it too well Chencho el Mocho'd called Manuel and Chacho cowards earlier on that day listen he said if you can't play these games like men shut up he'd said and if you can't hack it go fight like men too not like a couple of fags well after that they shook hands and said sorry and I'm telling you

all this in flashback so's you'll understand how things got to
such a pass well it starts with Manuel calling out hey Chacho
only he calls him Chango because it's easier to think of a
rhyme something about mashing Chango's mango and then
Chacho comes back go to hell Manuel and some filthy stuff
always rhyming well they got more and more insulting and
Chacho began to get very nasty making Manuel very red
when he said a donkey dipped its wick in a cup and Manuel's
mother licked it up so Manuel says the first thing that comes
to him he says remember the fellow called Dave who kept a
dead whore in a cave well I kept another and she was your
mother and Chacho shouts my Dad was a decent gent and my
mother a good respectable lady and you're just a son of a
bitch and your mother was a real whore hey hey hey they all
call out that doesn't rhyme that's cheating it might not rhyme
says Chacho but it's true enough see what I mean these poor
guys get so up tight over these goddam stupid games they're
capable of killing each other the poor have a right to amuse
themselves after all but this kind of thing can leave their poor
old parents without sons.

Home again after another hard day at a lousy job that wears
down your resistance and breaks your spirit. Brother Fidel's
almost exhausted but he still has enough energy to talk,
he loves a good discussion and although he pretends to be
shocked, he's the first to turn the conversation toward those
topics; what's more the guy's got a good sense of humor. The
heat burns us like the fires of hell. For my part, though, I've a
wonderful gift, a bit complex but wonderful nonetheless, for
I at one and the same time live on several planes and to deny
me this would be going against the very spirit of free ubiqui-
tous thought. I refuse with all the rebellion I can muster to
obey any absurd dictates of time and space that would limit
my multiple dynamics and oblige me to live and move in one
dimension! These days two very different tasks in very different places occupy my time, in addition to my family life, of
course, which also involves my presence. At night I take up

my pen and wander as a stranger among events of the past. Not that I scorn everyday reality, but should some greater power or my own whim demand, I am also transported to the future. Our physical energy alas has limits more confining than frontiers to our will, all the more so when its comforts have been denied for a time. About as well I'm due for a break soon.

There you go again you're like a broken record, man. Another night without sleeping. How are you, night owl? If this goes on you're going to die on us, enough is enough. Greetings, brother preacher, as it happens I'd calculated ten weeks to finish this book and send it to a competition some professors who teach Spanish are holding, it's at a university far, far away and bears the name of the Cosmoletters Competition, no less. Heavens above! even though you're nothing but one prime collection of dumb ideas and do nothing but talk talk talk crazy things, some of them going too far, I'm sorry for you man, you've got more than one screw loose. Now what are you doing? Why are you tearing up everything you've written? I read it again, brother, and it's all right for a first draft of a first attempt at writing Spanish the way it's spoken around here, but that's all. The pathos is overdone. Thirteen pages and the subject's killed my intellectual capacity. I'm only the referee, the impartial judge, and I hereby decree these pages go into the trash. The narrator's pontificating again, and that's flirting with demagoguery, it doesn't ring true. Nobody can set the world right by preaching, if you'll excuse me, only the metaphor is the faithful witness to human events; let mine be an example and the reader draw the conclusions. If a story shows things as they are, including those things that are hidden, it serves as a mirror and is a delight to all who read it. A watchman it might well be, brother scribbler, but what does all this writing earn you? What about all the years of hard work without seeing a cent for it? Don't come telling me it's the satisfaction that counts, because I see you getting angry at yourself at always having to make sacrifices so you can go on. It's you should be a preacher at my church, though you'd better wash your mouth out with soap and water first or cauterize it to get rid of all those dirty words. It is a duty, Fidel, one that I follow with a passion as a soul penetrating the flames; it pays with grief and distress. Riches might buy many things we desire, but there are other things which outlive time itself. All well and good writer-man, when it's a matter of faith, I believe what you say. Tell me though, hardhead, will you ever earn money with all this? In your own lifetime, I mean. Indeed, you'll see, without a crystal ball and mumbo jumbo, I'll tell you truths that none might deny, not in the slightest: I shall indeed publish more than ten books, teach in noble seats of learning, receive honors of great prestige and mock the ignoble dwarves by envy nourishèd, and what do you think of that brother preacher? There, I've burned my chorizo listening to you talking garbage. Now you listen to me before you burn your brain out . . . what's the use, though? There you are talking about the future, calm as you like. Indeed, I may not be a great writer but I know I have the spark of intuition granted to those who create. Huh, and that's what you tell the future with? More or less. In literature, time as we see it every day doesn't exist; past, present, and future dwell on the same plane in one dimension; in spite of their natural flow they can be described by the writer who contemplates them and reflects on them, reflects on them a great deal that is. Proud man, that power belongs to God alone! Listen here, you bargain basement theologian, God doesn't *think* at all. How can you say that, you idiot? Because God doesn't need to think, He's intuition itself. He knows all by merely looking; He doesn't have to think because He hasn't any doubts that need clearing up. Deductive reason would be wasted on Him. He constantly intuits and creates universes and all that exists. The stars in the sky bear witness to the greatness of His creation, on earth the rivers, mountains, and the seas are the work of His hand. And we have been granted a spark of His grace; we the poets are as little gods. You scare me brother, you anger me and scare me, and what's more, my potatoes have burned too from my listening to you. If you know all about the future tell me then what's going to happen to me? Will I be physician of bodies and souls? Will I be some great genius of theology? Will there be statues to me? ha ha ha. Come on, tell me, what do you say'll happen to my family and me—I'm only playing along, understand, you won't get a cent out of me for your fortune telling. Come on now . . . I'm ready. Let me calculate, you're twenty-three, married for five years, four children . . . seven and twenty-five make . . . Right! Got it! Do you love your wife, Fidel? Indeed I do, with all my heart, with all my soul, with all my strength, she's good and beautiful and a good Christian like me. He gave her to me, the Lord's name be praised. And do you love your children? With all my soul as the Lord our God loveth us. Right then, this is what's going to happen to you: in thirty-two years you'll have left your wife who's ugly and wrinkled, old and ill. Silence, sinner! You're crazy anyway! As for your children, you won't see them or their children, your grandchildren. You'll leave all behind and run off with a lovely twenty-year-old more adept in the arts of love than the queen of Sheba herself! And I've never heard such bunk! Ah, but the two of you will go live on an island far away. And there, friend, you'll die, alone, and your eyes will be dry of tears, for you'll have no more left to shed. You don't have the right to insult me like that! You're nothing but a miserable hack and you'd better say you're sorry! Ah, my friend, I'm afraid I can't, for it's already happened. How can you be so sure? Because, you see, I'm writing in flashback. You really are the limit! Indeed, I'm writing this in 1991. Still, Fidel, you and I will have to wander through these pages, laboring in industry and construction, because in fiction we're still in 1953. Well, I don't understand your crazy arguments and I don't want to. You're just playing a game with me because I don't understand anything about literature and dynamos and flashers' backs and heaven knows what else, you're just doing it to drive me crazy too. Brother, give time its time, the sad side of my own life will get its due when I write a novel that's mostly autobiographical, don't worry, I'm making notes already. Don't give me any more of these devil's games. Not a word more, and off to work we go. Since we've only been with this construction company for four days we've still a lot to learn about the guys we work with, one should always try to get to know them well, wouldn't you say? I say you like those rough toughs and you ought to live according to God's word, that's what I say, and I'm his humble servant.

Here we are so to work to work gird up the loins and all that yeah ours not to reason why so hustle your horse and don't say die 'scuse me a word with you I wanna talk to you about the boys in the gang hullo hullo old man what's all this what do you know about these things he he he don't they say the devil knows a lot because he's old sure they do but you wouldn't make it to third base agewise next to the devil though it's strange how you sound like the folks back home you're too old to be doing this work you're going to get all dried up and keel over on your mat would it matter so much if I did not to me anyway listen old man life's fuckin' hard around here this is donkey work it'll take the skin off anybody this gang gets its kicks playing the hoodlum they don't have any alternative going in for sports costs more than they can afford so they fight with insults and who's to blame them every day building goddam palaces and having to live in shitty shacks sorry to interrupt your speech young man nah y'know what there's something about your expression it's like I knew you how old are you old man anyway same as you sixty-two same as you come on now I'm twenty-three I was born in 1930 what does that make me twenty-three who're you kidding well that might well be look here young 'un listen to what an old man tells you take care of yourself around these folk yeah listen who are you old man I can't remember you talk different ways just like I do sometimes you're a hick

from North Mexico now you're a Pachuco wise guy next
you're a Mexican American Pocho and when you've got your
tie on you sound like a teacher listen here I wanna tell you
what happened last week before our friend Fidel the preacher
got here what's this about *our* friend I like Fidel Castillo he's a
nice guy hey where did you learn his name eh must have
heard it somewhere what's it to you why so surprised doncha
trust me I speak anyway I feel like just like you though perhaps not as varied since you're the expert after all that's your
life's work what's that old man what do you know about my
life's work nah don't interrupt an old man and lemme tell you
about things I know here we are in the desert and those bastards go levellin' the scrub in front of us and keep findin' rat-
tlesnakes every day they find 'em the goddam sonsabitches
well one day they throw this snake at us and El Chicorriatas
half stuns it with a stick picks it up and what'd'ya know if he
doesn't stick it in the mortar mix that's goin' up on the hoist
to the guys layin' bricks up there still very much alive the
goddam snake so the guys who give out the materials one of
'em puts it half covered up on a mortar board and that great
massive Anglo guy looks like a goddam elephant the one
called Litterjoe bends over and stirs the mortar and up comes
the snake with its tongue out and the guy just passes out
with shock then they passed it to Sam the Black guy always
laughin' and yellin' and wavin' his arms makin' a lot of noise
hey come here Sam and move this table El Chicorriatas tells
him you're as strong as superman while the other guy's passed
out cold over there and we're fannin' him with a hard hat so
the Black guy picks up the table with these long arms he's got
and goddamit the snake comes up like it's goin' to kiss him
and he ducks to one side and runs off yellin' an' makin' such a
row you'd've thought it was a herd o' goats stampedin' well
who comes then but the Pachuco foreman with the engineer
the boss this Mister Adams and since he doesn't know what's
goin' on he just stands there next to the goddam snake and
about as well he's wearin' boots it bites him but just his pants

you should've heard him yellin' like an old woman it was
Chon del Cid killed it finally hit it with his spirit level and
squashed its head and it seems it was full of little snakes the
way the body kept on wrigglin' in the middle now El Chicorriatas grabbed the tail and went down in the elevator they
say he had the idea of throwin' it at that pretty little gringa
who runs the lunch wagon you know where the sides go up
and she useta sell hot food come an' get it she shows up just
then lots for all of you no need to fight tacos sandwiches meat-
burros bean-burros hotdogs anything you like made your tripes
fair chuckle nice little thing with these shorts God they were
tight you'd think they'd have split her but she's real nice to
everybody ugly ones too well I'll tell you while they're busy
doin' one thing or another that goddam sonofabitch El Chicorriatas goes and ties the snake round the steering wheel of
the lunch wagon and when all the men go back to work Marlene gets back in her van not payin' much attention a real
charmer she was wavin' at all her clients and admirers and
she felt somethin' soft on the steerin' wheel and passes out as
she tries to get out up comes the heavy in this film poses there
with his foot on her neck who else could it be but the devil
himself El Chicorriatas of course he sticks one hand under her
legs one round her neck and moves her into the shade but the
boys start collectin' up two bucks a head while she lies there
hiccuppin' and cryin' and they made two hundred bucks for
her she gave 'em her little smile as off she went in her wagon
you shoulda seen that asshole El Chicorriatas was he mad he
didn't like her bein' all that popular so he starts to bad mouth
her said he'd put his hand in her blouse felt up her tit and you
know where else when he picked her up said she was pissin'
and fartin' so it sounded like Villa's machine guns takin' To-
rreon laughin' at her the bastard then he takes off God knows
where but it wasn't the end of the snakes every day the guys
with the tractors find two or three and throw 'em into the
cars so when folks were goin' home they'd be lookin' into the
windows just in case more than four of us nearly had a fit

hearin' rattlin' under the seat or turn round and there's a
snake hey young man what's so strange whatcha lookin' at me
like that for all thoughtful like doncha like my story sure it's
a good story you tell it well . . . but you know I've got the
idea someone told it to me before same words same gestures
some time ago ah well I don't know how that could be it only
happened a week ago don't kid me old man tell me your name
your full name ah sorry who's calling me now Simon el Pela-
gallos that's who coming coming Chente tell me what's that
old man over there called hell I don't know ask his mother he
only came here today everybody calls him the old man the
foreman just asked us hey you guys which one of you assholes
brought that old coot cause you can just take him home
again tell him to get lost I don't want to see him again well I
do there's some things I want to ask him like who's buried in
Pancho Villa's grave I'll go get him then hey Chatunga I need
to go to the bathroom I wouldn't if I was you brother you
crap at your own risk round here if you do use the portapotty
the scuse-me thing the toilet watch out they're building all
around it and you gotta watch out the other day I was having
a crap and they start to throw bricks at it you should have
heard them hit the metal roof and sides scared the shit out of
me which was all right at the time but wait a while better to
do it in your pants than risk your life for a lousy crap better
alive smelling like a dead cat if you can hold out a while the
fuckin' bosses'll be here and you can go and they can't make a
row and throw things then or they'll fire them you gotta learn
how to wise up round here I'm telling you cause you're a
good guy yeah well it's Friday payday the day the eagle shits
let's go to La Matanza and cash our paychecks and while
we're there we'll have a few cold beers here these guys'll give
you a lift you know I don't go to La Matanza nothing to
worry about brother Fidel after I've been to La Matanza we'll
have a bite to eat and beddy byes real early okay right old
man you going to La Matanza too can a duck swim I want to
talk to you a while find out who I am and who you are well

if the old man isn't the devil incarnate who else can he be
bring us a couple of mother 'n childs and no backing out
what's that you want to know what's a mother 'n child see
there a big beer momma with its tequila chaser on the side
good you can order me one that's had twins tell you what
young man that Pachuco foreman really knows his job he
speaks English real good and plays dumb when he has to he
knows how to get on well with all the workers an' he's got me
talkin' like him too hey hey what's the matter with you you
were so talkative chirpy chirpy and now look at you all down
in the mouth I guess I'm a bit under the weather can't sleep at
night the truth is I'm none too lively I'm so tired I could sleep
for a month come on man liven up a bit your eyes look like
cloudy plastic yeah and these drinks are getting to me too I'm
seeing double already things are starting to float strange how
everything's hovering around me and all the yelling that's going on here have another drink it'll help nah tell you what
guys I'm going to talk to the old man seems to me I know him
from somewhere what you laughing at old man thinking of
your sins eh nah just waitin' for you how's your brother El
Che tell me hey how do you know my brother El Che how do
you know all these things you didn't ought to listen old man
just because I've had a few drinks doesn't mean . . . listen I'm
the one who creates what I write about see and you're going
too far and asking questions I don't put in your mouth . . .
come here look at me doncha remember I'm the guy from Sinaloa useta call you a Yaqui Hick and you what was it you
called me Culichi from Culiacan that's it ah Cruz Ramos
that's who you are say what's going on round here not much
I've just come back to recreate the atmosphere of the fifties I
like doin' it I remember how my folks from back then used to
talk what they used to say how they used to live all the things
we need to know to be the way we should be so we can tell
the new ones what it was like for everything will disappear if
we trust our tracks to the wind if you don't want things forgotten you have to make footprints that last you're still wri-

tin' then just the way you were doin' way back and workin' at
those lousy jobs that wear you out racin' about with them
heavy tools careful not to fall down and break your neck then
you started teachin' and worryin' about the students no man
it's too much work you gotta learn how to save your energy a
bit tell me Cruz how did you learn all that bah gossip's everywhere a little bird told me and what's more I'm only a step
from the other dimension and not even writers know what
happens there it's all speculation nothin' for sure you'll see is
all this really happening Cruz I haven't slept for umpteen
nights all I do is write write write to try to get this book
ready in time and then all this work in the sun during the day
without any protection and then the other work you mention
I'm worn out with a fever that's burning me right to the mar-
row and these drinks have got me scared you can't possibly
be here it's just me seeing things hearing things my mind's
wandering that's what it is no writer-man of the desert sands
you've got it wrong I'm the one who's hallucinatin' round
here I'm on my last legs at this moment about to kick the
bucket down in Mazatlan and if it hadn't occurred to me to
slip into your private cosmos I'd be dead already see I'd just
gone into my final delirium and whatta I find but the stuff
you're writin' eh all about my old workmates so what'd I do I
just crashed the party and joined 'em since I knew 'em all
anyway and guess what not one sonofabitch knew me sure I
didn't ask you if I could come but here I am sixty-odd and
laughin' at your books and all the bullshit you believe about
bein' the boss as far as what you write's concerned hell man
right now I'm down there with my wife and kids back home
and I do believe I'm at the last gasp somethin' just happened
didn't you hear 'em all start to yell yeah there's Venustiana
havin' a fit and me goin' into a delirium sonofabitch that's
odd I'm in a wood with lots of dry trees huge trees all lined
up and not one goddam leaf I couldn't make a cup of tea if I
wanted one all very odd where the hell am I what happened
to the horse eh look at this these damned plants they all look

like letters very bad handwritin' though who's the asshole
wrote this t like a cross in a cemetery it isn't worth touchin'
wood for now here's a capital B with a nice round naked ass
like a beauty queen from Miami from Acapulco yes you're
Cruz Ramos all right the same guy I knew still laughing at
everything if I didn't know you were dying I'd give you a kick
up the ass ah would you and to show me if I'm a goddam immaterial being or not immaterial asshole that's what you are
it must be a dream a figment of a dream something from a
work of fiction sure I'm a figment spiritual to the core don't
change Culichi Cruz don't change listen writer-man the trees
were all in lines and I began to read I found out about Fidel
and the girl he ran off with the tale all about his death they
always did say two tits pull more than a tractor and a twat
can stop a train poor guy poor preacher man who knows perhaps he's back with you even now drivin' you crazy and you
him poor old Cruz your family must be upset don't kid yourself they put on a good show though there they are now fightin'
like hell over a few skinny cows that look more like scaffoldin'
a few things worth nothin' a few rags not worth the price of
aspirins to calm 'em down ask your friend the preacher Fidel if he remembers the fifty bucks I lent him and useta ask
him for all the time and whenever I did he'd quote the Bible
back at me I'm beginning to doze Cruz my eyes are closing
I'm falling asleep hell man I'm dyin' my soul's hangin' by a
goddam thread haven't you seen me nippin' out to take a leak
every minute or two do you think I'm goin' to check to see if
I'm still alive don't make me laugh you're seein' me checkin'
up on my last moments there in a room in my house with my
kids and the old woman all with long faces hell they look
worn out heartbroken they're wonderin' how much longer
I'm goin' to take to die I've been at it day and night listen to
my buddies outside tunin' their ears he was a good man it's
about time he went what's the bastard waitin' for there'll be
nothin' to drink at the wake the spiked coffee's growin' mush-
rooms already and why's that because I crashed your goddam

story that's why without so much as by your leave heh heh
gimme a drink of that pig's piss and be damned that's Cruz
Ramos he's dyin' and still cussin' that's right if we're screwed
we're screwed that's the way I talk I never stole from nobody
never killed nor poisoned though some deserved it did right
by all and I'm dyin' at peace and not all do there are those
who speak all fine and clean and nearly faint at a bad word
but they're storin' food to make a profit and lyin' for gain and
while I'm about it I might as well tell you for your information that Boni got his comeuppance in California in nineteen
eighty shot in the forehead like a pig in the stockyard Dogface
is still draggin' his ass around down there but a lot of the others are doin' the same up here I'm tellin' you just for the hell
of it like you write shit all the time that's how it is Death
came and got 'em and would you believe it El Chicorriatas
went and married the girl with the lunch wagon look at 'em
all dancin' to the jukebox like a pack of acrobats and some of
'em have arthritis now and more pains than a pig's whiskers
remember Fernando the spoiled brat he died sittin' on the sofa
and his old woman natterin' you never answer when I talk to
you Fernando you never pay attention answer when I talk to
you and him gettin' cold and I've got to run or I'll piss my
pants hey there buddy I'll take you home you're falling asleep
this is Boni the pinto pony remember we'll go in the Hare's
car and here's the old goat Chivo Reyes we'll be home in a
minute we're giving you a lift since you're a nice guy a bit
odd but nice enough we see you talking to yourself lonelylike
and when you get mad it isn't with malice and your lies always make us laugh here take my hand so you don't fall flat
Fidelito your buddy's arrived a bit stewed give us your hand
take care be seeing you brother well aren't we doing nicely
mister author got an escort to get him home but man you're
burning up you've gotta see a doctor here's a coffee and some
aspirins for the time being you should have been there Fidel
when I went to give my class this morning the students were
downright starry eyed they came up to congratulate me aren't

you proud teach' you being Mexican they've given Don Octavio Paz the Nobel Prize and the Chicanos all hugging and
shaking hands with me and each other you should have seen
and what you've got is delirium brother all the crazy useless
things you've learned from your foolish books if you stuck to
the Good Book things like that wouldn't happen to you Fidel
Fidel don't play dumb pay Culichi Cruz Ramos the fifty bucks
you owe him how can I if I don't know where he is how do
you know I owe him fifty bucks let me tell you brother and
don't call me a liar there's another writer a big cheese if you
like who visited me and it only seems like yesterday Don
Camilo José Cela and very friendly too me a hick from Sonora
Mexico so what says he I was a hick from Galicia too take a
couple of aspirins and sleep on it you're talking about people
and places that don't exist never did either poor guy I always
said you'd a screw loose brother in Christ Fidel good night
and God forgive our pride yours and mine may your soul rest
in peace as his eye is on the sparrow and if you want to know
I only stayed so long in the past preterite because old Cruz
from Culiacan was dying and wanted me to go with him good
old Culichi and you're up the pole Cruz Ramos isn't an old
man he's young like us tomorrow Fidelito when we wake it
won't be in this place you'll end up in Hawaii in the silent
groves of Necropolis with nobody to bug you nor tempt you
with galloping King Solomon's disease we'll jump ahead
thirty-eight years and I'll be an old teacher without a black
hair to my name blind as a bat and pulled by the force of
gravity till I walk with my eyes on the ground all right all
right yes man anything you say shut up now and sleep you're
as stubborn as a mule and drunk to boot goodbye dear brother
goodnight you nut sleep tight and shut your trap and we'll see
if the fever passes there's nothing I can do about your other
problem though . . . goodbye . . . goodbye. . . .

My work shall have no final rounding off; its development
and end must imitate the chaotic indecision of outrageous
fortune just as our lives run their course unaided by the pre-

tensions of some scribbler with a will to omniscience. Yet my same arbitrariness is but pretension, too, the pretension of all who would break with what is given, furthering the cause of uncertainty while announcing a renewal, which, in the end, might only serve to despoil. As this tale was wrought I had before me the image of a river of words and sound babbling to overflowing with slang, underworld cant, dialect, the hybrids of languages that could not be more foreign and unalike, and all sucked into the linguistic whirlpools coming together, surfacing and drifting apart, speech where evolution has given way to revolution producing an amazing metamorphosis—a river of words surging from the source unbound by any banks. Our current means of communication and demographic phenomena have wrought unimagined change in time and space; these are the factors behind the dizzy course of our Spanish tongue and are viewed as arms of chaos by those members of learnèd institutions who have lost sight of the origin of our language, its vulgar birth, the bastard of Latin. Yes, a river of words with other linguistic streams adding wildly to the swell and its mad dynamics. Yet what could be more fascinating, more engrossing than to contemplate the wild unbound course of these rivers dragging all along, erasing what it chooses and imposing its own will on the landscape? It is one with all phenomena in that it abhors the static, no matter who bemoans that fact or might bemoan it in the future.

Yet those advocates of exclusivity—surely it cannot be mere coincidence that makes them also the guardians of privilege of power and riches—are seeing themselves outnumbered day-by-day by this unbounded growth of those same masses whose domain is but that of wretchedness, and who have been granted a mysterious grace and rare privilege by some gift of nature itself. They have been granted the right to be destroyers of language and forgers of new speech as they form new sounds, change old words and ancient structures, take on foreign words and give birth to the children of free relations between tongues. Who knows what other wonders, too, are wrought. Can this be the collective working of the human soul spurred on by some secret will to vengeance on the cruelties, lies, and injustice beyond imagination it has suffered? If this be true let it be proof that if fine speech and learnèd rules wish to reign, they must, above all, pay respect to the speech of humble folk, for it is in them that the glory of language is reflected, as indeed those very folk are the reflection of their Divine Creator.

Translated by Alita Kelley in consultation with the author.

TRANSLATOR'S NOTE: In the original Spanish two sections are entirely in the Pachuco argot of the 1950s and would be totally undecipherable to the average reader. The translator could, perhaps, render the effect of the original with a translation into hermetic African American argot, or Cockney rhyming slang, thus replacing the secret language of one oppressed minority group with that of another but also defeating the purpose of depicting Chicanos and no other group. We have chosen to offer a comprehensible version in more-or-less standard English and request the reader's cooperation in attempting to understand the effect of the original.

PAT MORA

The Dance Within My Heart

For a Southwesterner, early spring in the Midwest is a time
for jubilation. Another winter survived. Why, then, on a soft
spring Saturday would I choose to leave the dogwoods and
daffodils and spend my day inside museums?

Certainly, I didn't spend my youth enduring trips through
solemn rooms, being introduced to "culture." There was only
one small art museum in my hometown, and I'm not sure
how comfortable my parents would have felt there. My father
worked evenings and weekends to support the four of us and
to give us what he and my mother hadn't had, a youth without financial worries. And my mother not only helped him in
his optical business but was our willing chauffeur in addition
to assisting the grandmother and aunt who lived with us, our
extended Mexican American family.

But as an adult I began to visit those echoing buildings.
A fellowship allowed trips to modest and grand museums in
New York, Paris, Washington, Mexico, Hawaii, and the Do-
minican Republic. And much to my surprise, I even found
myself directing a small university museum for a time, having
the opportunity to convince people of all ages and back-
grounds that indeed the museum was theirs. I was hooked
for life.

For me, museums are pleasure havens. When I enter, my
breathing changes just as it does when I visit aquariums,
zoos, botanical gardens. These latter sites offer a startling array of living species. Unless we have become totally desensi-

tized to nature's grandeur, to its infinite variations, arboretums and nature centers inspire us to treat our planet with more care, to be more attentive to the life around us, no matter how minute. I stand entranced by the spriteliness of glass shrimp, the plushness of the jaguar, the haughtiness of birds of paradise in bloom. Parrots make me laugh, fins spin my blood, ferns hush my doubts. I leave refreshed.

When they were younger, my children could far more easily understand my desire to visit displays of living creatures than they could my penchant for natural history and art museums, for gazing at baskets and pottery, at sculpture and flashing neon. It sounded like work walking through room after room, up and down stairs, being relatively quiet, not eating, reading small cards of text, staring at "weird" objects. This is fun?

But museums remind me of the strength and inventiveness of the human imagination through time. They remind me that offering beauty to a community is a human habit, a needed reminder in a society with little time for observing, listening, appreciating. I gaze at African masks crusted with cowrie shells, at drums and carvings of old, wrinkled wood, at the serenity of Buddha. I watch my fellow visitors, drawn to cases both by the beauty and craft but also as a kind of testimony to humans who once sat under our sun and moon and with rough hands graced our world.

I walk on to see the sturdy pre-Columbian female figures from Nayarit, Mexico, women of broad dimensions who occupy space rather than shrink as we sometimes do. I see pan pipes and bone flutes from Peru, 180 B.C., back then, high in the Andes, hear a man transforming his breath into music.

Room after room I watch light and shadow play on sandstone, silver, wood, bronze, earthenware, copper, ivory, hemp, oil, acrylic, watercolor, straw, gold. I study toenails on a headless marble statue, watch light stroke the soft curves, wish I could touch her outstretched Roman hand. The next room, or turning a corner, can yield surprise, the halls and rooms a pleasure maze. I stand in Chagall's blue light, see his glass bird poised to fly from room to room.

I ignore the careful museum maps, enjoying the unexpected, the independence of viewing at will, the private pleasure of letting myself abandon order and logic room to room. Purposeless wandering? Not really, for I now know I come not only for the intellectual and sensory stimulation but for comfort. I come to be with humans I admire, with those who produced these drums and breathing dancers, who through the ages added beauty to this world. Their work gives me hope, reminds me that art is not a luxury: it nourishes our parched spirits. It is essential.

I think again of how privileged I am to be in these quiet rooms, not having to wait for a free day, having time to spend wandering these galleries rather than having to care for someone else's children while mine are alone, or having to iron clothes that I will never wear.

And certainly free days and increased public programming—the democratization of museums—are an improvement from past eras, an acknowledgment, although sometimes grudgingly, that not only the "washed and worthy" deserve entrance. Museums are slowly changing, realizing that artifacts and art belong to all people, not some people. Museums are even becoming a bit embarrassed about how they acquired what they own, about why they arrogantly ushered certain groups past their polished doors. The faces viewing with me have been more varied in recent years.

I walk on. I, who can barely sew a button, study an array of quilts, glad that such women's art is now displayed, think of the careful fingers—stitch, stitch, stitch—and probably careful voices that produced these works. The text of a bronze of Shiva says that her dance takes place within her heart. I study her and think of that dance, of the private nature of that spring of emotion. I watch a group of teenage girls walk by and wonder if they can hear or feel their private dance in a world that equates noise and brutality with entertainment.

The contemporary art halls most baffled my children when they were young. "Why, I could do that!" they would scoff staring at a Jackson Pollock. I smile secretly when my youngest, now taller than I am, asks, "Where are our favorite rooms?" meaning, yes, those rooms with massive canvases, with paint everywhere, the rooms that loosen me up inside, that provide escape from the confines of the predictable.

I walk outside glad to breathe in sky and wind but also brimming with all I saw and felt, hearing the dance within my heart.

PESCADOTE

What think you, Old Fish,
mammoth, mud-stuck
for centuries, your scales
released long ago
like tiny chimes beckoning
fishermen who slipped the silver
under their pillows,
dreamed of swimming
with huge starfish
in the soft night sky.

What think you, Old Fish,
your flesh nibbled
by hungry river breezes
that licked even your wild
eyes away, your moon-white bones
thickening, expanding
with wet burrowings, fins
and tendrils skimming your ribs,
roots curling into your damp crevices.

What think you, Old Fish,
spiders lacing your gray crust,
spinning their slow stories
on you, lone river island
unmoved by torrents,
trees sprouting from your head,
in late afternoon humming,
your mouth open wide
to the gathering wind.

JOEL HUERTA

Gardenia

In the year 1969, two blocks of what used to be a carrot field, then an onion field, then a carrot field again, became Memorial Park (what it memorialized was never quite clear). Silver, red, and blue. Space theme. An aluminum rocket with a steep and spiraling slide, a flying saucer, spotted space creatures on truck springs, a barbecue pavilion, little league and tennis—a decent American implementia for coming of age.

We were a few months away from the seventies, when "the sixties" finally arrived in our town. Someone faraway had made a decision in our favor. "All in favor of helping these little folks say Ay."

"Ay!" and it was done.

A new pretend-wood government trailer pulled up next to Reyna's Neighborhood Grocer and stayed for over a year. The sign on it was red, white and blue, a hands-shaking-hands inside the silhouette of a house type of logo. It was Urban Renewal.

The information was posted outside in English *and* Spanish. I remember people scratching their heads in awe. "Spanish. El Tío Sam speaks Spanish? I mean, who woulda thunk?"

Most of the younger folks sort of understood the English. The Castillian Spanish with its "vosotros" and such was far more confusing. It was, however, the *gesture* of having Tío Sam give a damn for a change. Yes, someone faraway had acknowledged our existence. They had gone through the effort and expense to include us. Imagine the sudden transcendence in our status, in their *perceptions* of our status—if the govern-

ment couldn't fully communicate with us because of language, it was perhaps their shortcoming, not ours. The wolf,
which for years had been hunted, was now on some list of
the endangered. Without parade or ceremony, the ribbon
had been cut. Welcome to western civ you little *Tejanitos!*

Like Noah's select beasts walking two and two into the old
ark, my father the mechanic, and my mother, farmworker
turned housewife turned florist, found themselves, along with
the rest of the neighborhood couples, heading to the Urban
Renewal trailer.

They met with the Urban Renewal people, had interviews,
meetings, reviews; received free legal advice and counseling
on how to get a good loan; and talked about the future.

"The future?" Who could afford the future? Our barrio lived
paycheck to paycheck. Sunday barbecue to Sunday barbecue.
Even people in Appalachia saw us "Mexican folk" on Walter
Cronkite's evening news and pitied us.

* * *

I remember sitting on the steps of Reyna's store (cold-cut loafs
and longhorn cheese and a barrel of pickles, sawdust on the
floor). There I waited for my parents to return from their
meetings. I'd get my quarter and with that I'd buy a pack of
Tom's peanuts to pour into my RC Cola bottle. The pleasure
was to eat a few softened peanuts every time you drank. We
called these cocktails "goober cokes."

Sitting on those steps with my goober coke, my little green-
house of a brain constructed and outfitted a house much bigger, more sober—pilasters behind a balustrade—of course,
much more than we could afford then, than I can afford now.

Soon after the Urban Renewal trailer showed up, poly-
ester men came calling, peddling blueprints to cheapo houses
which most of our neighbors would end up taking. My parents would sneer at the suckers—*raza, pura raza.* Some folks
just couldn't change.

Mom and dad perused the Sunday classifieds. Since my

mom had become a florist, she had become quite particular about dos and don'ts in decor of the middle class. Her job occasionally took her into some very nice homes. She set the ground rules for ours.

We must have some paneling, but absolutely not *dark* paneling. Wallpaper in the kitchen and bath. Closed garage. Central air conditioning. No colors, only grays, creams, and whites.

When it came time to shop for a lot or an acceptable house, we drove through every neighborhood on the nicer west side of our South Texas town. Most of the time we were humbled by the lawns spread like aquamarine rayon bibs before the sealed-off houses.

As we shopped for our new life, we were checked by the glances of the middle class. We were, afterall, a "Mexican" family crammed into a GMC work truck pointing and gawking at them.

It was a cloudy day when we found the site in the Gardenia Subdivision, Garza Street. It was probably fall. A lone boy punted a football, then sprinted out to try and catch it. A perfect place. Ours became the seventh or eighth home to be built. Now there are some twenty-five houses. It's what realtors call "a pride of ownership" neighborhood.

Gardenia was and remains all brown. *Tejanos.* Mostly teachers and foremen and clerks at the nicer stores, and Gardenia does have a lawyer, and a school principal, and an entrepreneur or two. It has its sprinklers and Hondas. Its joggers, Walkmans, pet-store pets pulling on the leash, yellow ribbons, and floodlit Old Glories waving during the little war.

And Gardenia has had its tragedies—suicide, cancer, rumors of homosexuality, and it has its longer list of triumphs—children who leave and return home in new cars, satellite dishes, second-generation Gardenians building their own new houses, honors, great *pachangas*, employee-of-the-month commendations, and the occasional photograph in the "Lifestyles" section of the *Edinburg Daily Review*.

In less than a year after the Urban Renewal trailer showed up, we were ready for a new home. We owned a half acre of America.

Even before ground was broken, we'd go every other day to see it. We would poke around in the weeds, wild sunflowers, and Bermuda grass. "We'll put a cactus garden here, a citrus tree there, mailbox over there."

When ground was finally broken for the house, we checked on the progress daily. With just the foundation down, our Great Society house seemed tiny, the size of a play castle. It was important to boast of owning a four-bedroom home, so space that would have made two comfortable bedrooms, made four cubicles we'd learn to live with.

And the lot was too big and untamable—three hundred sunflower weeds—a legacy of yard work for all of us. And there were trees to be bought and planted, and we'd need to buy a walkway and a driveway, and where could we get a half-acre's worth of sod? And what about appliances and decent furniture? Oh, and appropriate school clothes? And a birdbath? Our American dream began.

In a few years our family wedged itself into the middle class, but there was tremendous cost. My father worked from 6:00 A.M. to 8:00 or 9:00 or 10:00 P.M. *and* moonlighted on weekends. I really wish this were an exaggeration. My mother did essentially the same, and we were still, we were afraid, always the poorest little family in the Gardenia Subdivision.

We were located a bit far from town and at first there were no kids on the block. Summers were the worst. Because we needed to appear prosperous to our neighbors, my mother made me keep the house windows shut. You see, in our town there were two kinds of neighborhoods, those with air conditioning and those without. Our old neighborhood—Yucatán Street—had been a neighborhood of wide open doors and windows with ripped screens. Yucatán Street was a cacophony of roosters and radios and yelling at children; tortillas, eggs, and beans wafting from one kitchen to the next, and love talk in the middle of the night, and creaking bedsprings at midday, *colorful*, a Texan Macondo.

Gardenia homes were sealed off and modern, all electric, and personalized—no two houses had the same type of brick.

Because we couldn't afford to run the air conditioning during the day when my parents were off at work, we had to look like we did. Set just a bit north of the Tropic of Cancer, our ranch colonial got terribly hot and stuffy and lovely. We had champagne-colored drapes and silk flower bouquets everywhere, and some half dozen flower sachets to mask the stink of new paint. The place could shut in on you like a lid on a coffin.

I think we were happy. The Gardenia Subdivision for us became the promised "Great Society." We owned a lawn so plush you could sleep on it. We had cars and vocations of which to be proud. Our Great Society was middle-class and American. We were a might closer to equality. I could say (even to white kids, who in South Texas were always better off), "This is my house," and then they'd have to like me.

On Yucatán Street the only way out of poverty (realistically) seemed through brokering marijuana for the college towns of the north.

With the tax-free marijuana profits, a *vato* could put away a decent stash so that when the other *vatos* decided to carve out his guts or when the DEA locked him away in Huntsville, his wife, mother, and kids could live off the grocery bagsful of twenties.

* * *

As I write this, I'm looking at the picture taken at my sixth birthday bash on Yucatán Street. I'm standing between my two best friends, Rudy and Roel. Last I heard Rudy was a coke junkie living with his father; Roel is a red-car-driving dealer, living high. And the birthday boy here, in the green glow of his word processor, is trying to convince himself with this confession, with this affirmation: "I am a survivor."

Oh, and I forgot Eddie, there at my party on Yucatán Street. He's the one standing behind us with the enormous slice of cake. Last year, Eddie shot his boy, then shot himself.

And there was Manche, who isn't in the picture, but who was at my party, picking his ear with a little plastic fork behind my grandmother, the photographer.

Manche, who married at sixteen. Who got into drugs. Who committed suicide with his fourteen-year-old bride after a football game we had won. Adrift on heroin, they dressed in black. They walked hand in hand down the middle of Canton Road and just like that they were gone. Hit. Killed by a Lincoln Continental in the hands of a tipsy "lady of the night."

These were the kids who helped me smash open my piñata.

In Gardenia most of the children survived. They were expected to attend a vo-tech school or President Johnson's gift to our community: the modern and new Pan American University with a planetarium, performing arts center, dormitories, four-storied library with microfiche, abstracts, the works. All of this just a mile away from home.

Grown Gardenia kids lived at home. They worked part-time. They'd buy a new truck or a Firebird Trans Am, perhaps. They would reserve a little extra money for socializing at Bocaccio 2000 or the Sheraton's Club Dallas. Eventually, there would be weddings.

Indeed, we had come quite far. Despite what Ronald Reagan called "a long and sorry tale of disappointment," the large government programs of the post-Eisenhower years were not a failure. Not to us. For my family and many like us, a decent, not a "Great," society did coalesce. Our real disposable income did not grow by 24 percent as it did for the average American in the period of 1965 to 1972, but it did grow. And that little shift in economic status had cultural ramifications as well. We became galvanized. We were not just Mexicans anymore, we were Mexican hyphen Americans.

I mean, my mother tells stories of being sprayed by agribusiness crop dusters while she and her brothers worked the fields. The machinery of progress had made her expendable. The Great Society initiative made her visible—made her officially American.

The gift of the Great Society was not money; it was simple acknowledgment, *recognition*. Granted, for a number of families in our old barrio Urban Renewal did nothing but make them bitter about leaving their homes for "a gringo neighborhood." And if tonight you and I were to go out and knock on the front doors of those folk's homes, I'm afraid we would find that many of them simply packed up their squalor and unpacked it somewhere else. Nothing but the view out of their windows changed.

Though my parents had to scratch and claw to maintain status quo in Gardenia, my parents did it gladly, selflessly. Dignity and good ol' materialism are potent pills. Imagine, within a decade, the America that had all too often turned up their noses at mom, dad, and their children, for being who we were and who we weren't, that America had had to become kinder, gentler. Though we still lived paycheck to paycheck, in our new life the checks were a bit bigger and the victories sweeter. Dad paid cash for his former landlord's hardly used white on white Cadillac Sedan de Ville. A small triumph. My siblings and I all went to college, and so forth. The rest of the story is much like yours. That's the point.

In 1969 we got a little break. If the white knight hadn't been big government, it may have been big business. Perhaps, a high-tech firm with a fat government contract would have come to our predominantly Chicano South Texas town and offered Señor and Señora X good jobs with HMOs, retirement, and benefits.

They didn't. Those companies went to better hometowns with better schools, better parks, better views. They went to you.

GABRIEL OLVERA

VOICE

At school my voice is a plain
the soil of northern terrain
a great field of monotone days
flatland from October to May.

At home it is a row of hills
a southern sierra regaining color
or a Mexican range come every summer
my voice from June to September.

EASTSIDE AFTERNOON

It's an Eastside afternoon
and our sister is masterpiecing
like Frida in our yard
where she has dad
being keen on high fruit
and mom seeding
loofahs under the sun,
has us strolling Broadway
through Chinese toy shops
Iranian food marts
and the sidewalks
selling snow (on a cone)
to catch the kite above the park

to greet the Saturday steeple
¿Qué hubo?

It's a quarter after two
as the people pour the water
on the baby's head
red and crying
and the girl with fifteen
blooms on her dress
is a woman smiling, laughing
and the bride and groom
are kissing and dancing
around tables of *mole*
past the warm *pozole* for that
sweet *atole* under the trees
toasting this Eastside afternoon
this masterpiece.

HUG

Grandfather,
you feel
like a fig tree rooted
in firm Mexican soil
hummingbirds
gathered round
breathing
your purple lore
sipping acoustic nectar
from the heart
of your grand-flower,
your life.

MARÍA HERRERA-SOBEK

EL CAMBIO DE LA GUARDIA

Casas inglesas
La lluvia inglesa
Un jardín inglés
Pan y mermelada
Acento "Cockney"
Por las calles
De la estación de Earle
Londres.

Observa
La cara café obscura
Grita
Y otra
Y otra
Pakistanos
En busca de algo
Mujeres hindus
En sus saris
Sonríen

El mundo gira.

THE CHANGING OF THE GUARD

English townhouses
The English rain
An English garden
Scones and marmalade
Cockney accents
On the streets
Of Earle Station
Londontown

You look
A brown face
growls
And another
And another
Pakistanis
On the prowl
Indian ladies
In their saris
Smile

The world does change.

LA REINA ELIZABETH

La reina Elizabeth
No sale
Sin tener
Su guardia de honor

Con ametralladoras
Los Soldados Reales
Un carro blindado
Y blindadas las ventanas
Para protegerla
No del sol inglés
Sino de la brillante
Explosión
De una bomba

QUEEN ELIZABETH

Queen Elizabeth
Does not step out
Too lightly
She needs
An honor guard
A machine gun
Toting Royal Soldier
A leaded car
And leaded windows
To guard her
Not from the English sun
But from the bright
Explosion
Of a bomb.

OAXACA III

Oaxaca
existes
entre la fina neblina
que cubre tu cara
como velo de novia.

Mañana
cubriré mi frente
con el jasmín
de tu recuerdo.

OAXACA III

You exist
Betwixt the fine gossamer fog
That lightly caresses your forehead
Like a bride's veil.

Tomorrow
I will cover my forehead
With the sweet jasmin scent
of your memories.

ROWENA A. RIVERA

El improvisador Casimiro Mendoza

Bueno, ya que hay tantas versiones de la vida de don Casimiro, todas equivocadas, claro, aquí les voy a contar la verdadera historia del mentado Casi, que recientemente murió,
Dios en paz lo tenga. Pos ya sabrán que en toda su larga vida
gozó de una reputación muy especial; de joven fue un carpintero requetebueno y hasta le dio por ser santero y después
pasó a ser uno de los escrividores públicos del pueblo y ya, de
hombre maduro, se convirtió en adivino, brujo y consejero de
todos los que hartos de la vida, enfermos del alma, llegaban a
su pequeñita casa a buscar alivio a sus penas. A causa de los
estraordinarios y legendarios sucesos de su vida, el pueblo le
atribuyó mala fama. Dicían, y aún siguen diciendo, que era
un embustero, un farsante, un fanfarrón y un mentecato, pero
otros juran que era un buen curandero, hombre sabio y espiritual y el mejor médico en estos lugares. Alto, flaco, de largos
brazos y piernas, un poco jorobado, miope con lentes peque-
ños y gruesos, parecía un pájaro raro cuando de joven cru-
zaba a largos pasos la plaza, fumando y leyendo, como siempre,
o con una mirada penetrante y lustrosa, su mente en otro
mundo. Aunque nunca se casó, dicían todos que siempre estuvo enamorao de una que otra, de esa soltera, de aquella
viudita, y hasta de vez en cuando peligraba su vida a causa
de su atención especial a esa hermosa casada que llegaba allí
a la plaza donde se ganaba la vida escriviendo cartas o a su
casa para solicitar sus variados servicios.
    Miren, a mí me tocó oír a los viejitos contar que de joven
Casimiro se dedicaba a construir hermosos muebles de pino,

labrándolos con todo un arte florido de pajaritos, angelitos, corazones, florecitas y no sé qué más. También, como resultao de algún arrebato espiritual, o de alguna necesidá económica, tallaba, por encargo, santos como San Judas Tadeo o para las mujeres, santas como la Santa Bárbara, que según entiendo, fue en la historia la primera santa feminista, o algo así, no sé cómo dicen eso hoy en día. En esos años cuando Casi apenas tenía veinticinco años, se preparaba para su vida matrimonial, haciendo una casita de ladrio, construyendo hermosos muebles para casarse con Genoveva, una muchacha de una rara belleza—me tocó conocerla—de una mirada estraña, un poco bizca, que como todos cuentan, la hacía verse más erótica. Pero esa boda nunca tuvo lugar. Dos días antes del casorio, con todos los preparativos ya listos para la ceremonia, la hermosa Genoveva cayó muerta, dizque de un derrame celebral, dejando a Casi en la más negra y disesperada depresión y desilusión. Después del funeral, se metió a la cama y allí estuvo tirao por seis meses, sin deseos de hacer nada, sólo quería morir—a mí me dijo—ya ni siquiera se preocupó por la casita recién hecha, los muebles—hasta dejó de ser carpintero—y sus padres tuvieron que vender o dar todo lo que tan amorosamente havía hecho por tan largo tiempo.

Ha de haver deseao la muerte tan intensamente que se le cumplió su deseo, o sea, dicen que se le cumplió. En la depresión que sufría, tuvo un ataque de miningitis, no sé cómo pronuncian eso, y quedó en un estao profundo de coma. Sus padres lo llevaron rápidamente al Hospital General en El Paso de donde lo trasladaron inconsciente, por avión, ya casi muerto, a San Antonio y después en otro avión a Houston donde havía famosos médicos que se especializaban en enfermedades del celebro. Todos los dotores pronosticaron la inevitable muerte del joven, y uno de ellos dio hasta el día esacto, la hora esacta en que Casi llegaría al final de sus días en este mundo. Los adoloridos padres, que un año antes havían sepultao a otro hijo, Azaleo, algunos de ustedes se acordarán de ese joven músico, no tuvieron otro remedio que traerlo al pueblo y llegó el pobre moribundo en ambulancia, camía y todo, ante los ojos compasivos de los vecinos. Se empezaron a hacer los preparativos para su inevitable muerte; llegó el sacerdote y le aministró los santos óleos, se empezaron a preparar los velorios, los rosarios y las esquelas y se les pidió algunos de sus amigos que escribieran los obituarios que se leerían en el funeral. Uno de los elogios más hermosos y emotivos fue escrito por don Salomón, el otro carpintero que, por cierto, nunca había querido a su talentoso competidor pero que en el obituario descrivía el trabajo de Casi en palabras bíblicas, descriviendo con mucha emoción, la entrañable amistá que siempre había unido a los dos carpinteros y santeros. Los padres y las vecinas arreglaron el cuerpo de Casimiro y lo pusieron en uno de los cuartos de la casa de sus padres que quedava allí mismo en la plaza por donde pasavan los amigos y vían el cuerpo largo, huesudo, con ojos cerradísimos, a toda vista, fuera deste mundo. Las mujeres se persinaban y se dicían, "se lo llevó la Genoveva, se lo llevó, ya recuerdas lo celosa que era," mientras que los hombres, al asomarse por la ventana y al ver su cuerpo completamente imóvil, se quitaban respetosamente el sombrero y bajavan la vista, aunque huvo unos que dicían, "Se está haciendo, si ya lo conoce uno, se ha estao haciendo to'o este tiempo."

Yo no podría decir si eso era cierto, pero lo que resultó fue que un sábado, temprano, 6 de agosto en la madrugada, justamente la fecha que los dotores habían señalao como el momento de la verdadera muerte de Casimiro, el joven abrió los ojos, y casi enojao, viendo a su alrededor a las mujeres llorosas con el rosario en la mano, dijo "¿Y qué carajos estoy haciendo aquí otra vez?" a lo que los cínicos esclamaron "¿No te dije? Se estava haciendo." Pos entonces se levantó Casimiro de la cama rodeada de velas, bueno y sano, no se imaginan, y después de bañarse para quitarse tantos polvos, aceites y ungüentos con que lo havía embadurnado la Felícitas, se sentó a comerse un enorme plato de fideos con carne y chile, y después se puso a leer sus obituarios, de vez en cuando sonriendo

socarronamente y hasta riéndose con una carcajada seca.
Quién sabe qué bicho le picó, pero dicen que a la siguiente
mañana salió con una mesita y una máquina antigua de escrivir, y se sentó a la sombra de unos árboles de la plaza a
esperar a que vinieran clientes a pedirle alguna carta, en inglés o en español, le dava a los dos, al gobierno federal pre-
guntando por algún cheque desvalagado, al alcalde de Las
Cruces para quejarse de los pésimos servicios médicos del
pueblo, a un pariente en México notificándole la enfermedad
y muerte de algún tío, tía, cuñado, y hasta escrivía peticiones
de matrimonio, que era lo que se hacía en esos años, como ya
recordarán, no como ahora, que nomás dicen nos casamos y
ya, nada de respeto por las costumbres bonitas de antes. Pero
lo que más le gustava a Casi era escrivir cartas de amor, y
claro, era lo que hacía mejor.

Yo todavía un chamacón, me tocó ver a Casi componer esas
cartas. Me iva los domingos por la mañana para havlar con
otros que se juntavan allí para esperar a que salieran sus mujeres de la misa y para havlar con los otros granjeros sobre las
condiciones deplorables de las acequias, el alto costo de los
fertilizantes y cosas de ésas. Frecuentemente, para divertirme
un poco me iva allá con Casi, que siempre tenía mucha clien-
tela que lo rodeava esperando su turno o que solamente ivan
a fisgonear, porque no hay que negarlo, el joven escrividor, en
los momentos de inspiración, de improvisación, cerraba, emo-
cionado, los ojos y dava rienda suelta a su imaginación, reci-
tando y escriviendo a la vez y claro, armaba todo un show
allí en la plaza . . . escéntrico, estrambólico que era Casimiro
en esos años. Pero no vayan a creer que así nomás se ponía a
escrivir. Primero les hacía un largo y complejo interrogatorio
a sus clientes, que casi siempre eran hombres que querían
mandarles a sus queridas, novias, esposas, algún versito, alguna declaración amorosa, que tal vez en persona no se atre-
vían hacer.

Pos ya se podrán imaginar, con la fama que tenía Casimiro,
lo que les preguntava a los hombres, y claro, lo que contestar-

ían algunos de los cínicos, burlones, porque empezava Casi a
querer saber que si de qué color tenía el pelo, los ojos, la piel;
que si era alta o chaparrita o si tenía labios anchos y sen-
suales, pestañas largas y sedosas, cuello esquisito, pies perfec-
tos, algunas señas particulares como un hoyuelo o un lunar, y
en qué lugar, o qué sueños tenía esa mujer o algo más secreto
que solamente el hombre podría saver, alguna tierna manía y
así seguían las preguntas. Lo que siempre preguntava era si la
mujer tenía los ojos un poco bizcos, y claro, siempre havía
alguien que contestaba que sí. Pos eso lo entusiasmaba muchísimo y lo llenava de un intenso amor. Y luego Casi, ya in-
spirao con tanto detalle, se ponía en su máquina a componer,
recitar y escrivir todo a la vez. Después se quedava con la co-
pia carbón y la otra se la dava al cliente que firmava su nombre
o hacía una crucecita, pagava unos dólares y el negocio quedaba hecho.

Allá al otro lao de la plaza, estava raviando don Secundino, que ya llevava añales travajando como escrividor del
pueblo y que vía cómo, día a día, Casimiro le quitava el negocio con sus esageraciones y el teatro que montava allí en
público. De tantas cartas de amor que escrivía Casimiro—algunas de las mujeres dicían que las cartas eran pura poesía,
que siempre las guardarían, mientras que otras no querían
que sus amantes o maridos se acercaran a Casi—llegó a cono-
cer muchos secretos y cosas ocultas de mujeres del pueblo, las
cuales empezaron a notar que algunas veces se quedaba mir-
ándolas, en cierto modo, en la estafeta, en las tiendas, en la
iglesia, como si supiera algo personalísimo de ellas, como si
estuviera enamorao de ellas.

Eso de ser escrividor empezó, como ya les dije, como di-
recto resultao de su rara esperencia en el otro mundo. Ahora
se le añadía otra leyenda a Casimiro: que havía muerto y re-
sucitao. Tanto le pedían que contara lo que havía visto y con
quién havía hablao cuando estava muerto, que al fin Casimiro empezó a organizar sesiones especiales, cobrándoles a

todos, claro, un dólar o dos, y se ponía a contarles de sus esperencias en ultratumba.

"Miren," les dicía, "recuerdo que primero vi un enorme círculo de luz resplandeciente que me envolvió completamente, llenándome de paz y calma, y me hizo subir, atravesando unos rayos fuertes de sol, a un lugar alto de donde se vían cuatro montañas, cada una en los cuatro puntos del mundo. Esa subida iva como a una piedra blanca, brillante, y vi a muchos conocidos por allí que me saludavan felizmente, se sonrían serenamente y que, al havlar con ellos, parecían estar enteraos de todo lo que pasa aquí en el pueblo. Hasta vi a mi hermanito Azaleo, pero todos eran Azaleo también, porque parecía que no havía diferencia entre todos los muertitos allá arriba. Yo buscaba a Genoveva. Bueno, al havlar con ella, o una de ellas, me saludó tan feliz que yo me sentí un poco enfadao porque se vía contenta, mientras que yo aquí he estao sufriendo día a día, hora a hora, por ella. Se lo reclamé y ella, calmadamente me dijo, "Si estás enojao o celoso, eso quiere dicir que toavía estás vivo, que estás destinao a volver al otro mundo. Así es que salúdame a mis padres." Yo apenas tuve tiempo de dicirle que sufría mucho por no estar con ella, que le dedicaría el resto de mi vida a escrivirle cartas de amor, que siempre la amaría el resto de la eternidá y que esperaría el día en que estuviéramos juntos de a de veras. Y ella me dijo, calladamente, "Ya olvídate, hombre, esa pasión no esiste aquí. Vuelve a tu destino."

Y eran tan estraordinarias las sesiones a las cuales, claro, Casimiro siempre añadía más y más detalles, que fue como empezó a ser, además de escrividor, consejero y adivino, ya que venían muchos a preguntar si allá en el mundo de los muertos havía visto a fulanito o a fulanita y que qué havían dicho y si havían preguntao por ellos. Casimiro contestava seriamente, "Allá tu mamá te está viendo hacer tanta burrada los sábados en la noche cuando te emborrachas." Y preguntava el paciente, "¿Está triste por eso? ¿Está sufriendo por mí?" Y Casi le dicía, viendo al paciente a los ojos, "Eres tú el que estás sufriendo. Eres tú el que está triste porque llevas un dolor adentro. Sácatelo."

Algunos seguían pensando que Casimiro era un enredador de mentiras, que el pueblo debía ignorarlo porque tal vez estuviera haciendo más daño que bien en esas sesiones de la muerte con los borrachales y después con los jóvenes que empezaron a atacarse de marijuana y drogas y todo eso que yo, ya de viejo, jamás he conocido. Ay tienes el caso de Benito, ¿se acuerdan? que por muchos años había sido alcohólico, como el San Benito, patrón santo de los borrachos, por quien había sido nombrao y que, como su santo, resultó completamente curao de su vicio.

"Y cómo, dime," le preguntaban a Benito, "¿Cómo fue que te curó ese viejo embustero?" "Pos no me dio más drogas como los dotores en Las Cruces y El Paso. Solamente con palabras me curó. Me ponía a recitar cuentos y poemas, y eso me curó." Y le contestaban, "No, hombre, eso no es posible. Te ha de haer dao algo." Y él les dicía, "No, no, te juro que fue así. Toavía me sé de memoria los poemas porque me los aprendí con el corazón y la mente. Me dicía Casimiro que repitiera lo que él dicía, como si él también estuviera buscando lo mismo que yo.

'Señor, si yo por mis limitaciones y flaquezas humanas me olvido a veces de tí, Tú, Señor, no te olvides de mí un sólo instante. Tú, que eres mi creador, sigue queriéndome para que yo aprenda a quererme también. Sigue creyendo en mí, para que yo aprenda a creer en mí. Creador mío, que me distes vida, ayúdame a vivir'."

"Repítelo," dicía don Casimiro. "Repítelo hasta que lleguen las palabras a los secretos de tu corazón, hasta que sean los alientos de tu alma. Repítelo cuando tengas ganas de irte con tus amigotes a la cantina, que es cuando estás sufriendo los dolores de tu mal. Y si toavía te quieres ir a tomar, acércate a las fuerzas de la creación, porque tienes que crearte de nuevo; ponte a serruchar leña para hacer muebles, santos; a construir casas, componer o cantar canciones, o hacer círculos o cuadros con lo que hay dentro de tu corazón y tu alma, y diariamente ponte a escrivir algún poema de amor, que es acercarte a los orígenes de la reproducción; y si toavía no brota tu verdadera pureza, agárrate entonces a un árbol y no te sueltes, ya que el árbol es el símbolo sagrado de la nueva vida." Y dicían algunos de los vecinos cuando vían a Benito, llorando, temblando de pies a cabeza y agarrao a un árbol, "Uuu, ese pobre ya está más loco que su maistro." En fin, así era como Benito descrivía el tratamiento y siempre les dicía a todos que lo que los dotores con tantas diplomas y lisensias en las paderes no havían podido hacer, Casimiro sí pudo. Claro, les diré que Casimiro no siempre tuvo éxito, por ejemplo, el caso reciente de Rigoberto, pero que como después dicían, el Beto no quiso hacerse una nueva vida.

Ya para este tiempo Casi solamente se dedicava hacer negocio con los hombres, curando solamente a hombres, y dejándole a la Felícitas las curaciones de las mujeres. Por cierto que se oyó, aquí y allí, las malas lenguas, que Casi y Felícitas, en unos tiempos lejanos, se vían juntos meditando y orando en el desierto, y sabrá Dios qué más haciendo y hasta se oyó el runrún de que él era el padre de Eduviges, hija de doña Feli. Pero nunca se supo definitivamente si eso era verdá o no. El hecho es que Felícitas, hierbera, partera y sobadora, y Casi, escrividor público, consejero y brujo, en cierta manera eran competidores en el mismo negocio y algunos dudavan de todos esos chismes. Cuando Casi toavía curaba mujeres, algo ocurrió, tan horrible, que desde ese suceso triste, jamás volvió a permitir mujeres en su casa. Además este evento doloroso produjo otro cambio en su vida personal.

Aunque hay muchos que cuentan diferente este caso, yo les digo la purita verdá porque a mí, personalmente, me lo contaron así: que un día una hermosa niña de quince años llegó llorando a la plaza y se sentó al lao de Casimiro que en ese entonces ya tendría sus cuarenta y pico de años. Entre sollozo y sollozo, lágrima y más lágrimas, hipos y más hipos, y agarrada del pañuelo de Casimiro, la niña le contó que la havía abandonao su marido, que la havía golpiao, que ahora no savía qué hacer, que no tenía dinero, que mejor quería morir. Casimiro, completamente embobao con la hermosura de la morenita de ojos verdes, cabello rizao hasta la cintura, no día nada, no savía qué dicir, pero al fin se recobró un poco y empezó a preguntarle algo de su situación matrimonial, de causas y efectos y todo eso. Después de varias conversaciones allí en la plaza, la niña, Raquel, así le dijo que se llamava, y Casimiro, se hicieron buenos amigos, y en cosa de unos diitas, una semana, o qué sé yo, la Raquelita resultó viviendo en casa de Casimiro, y los sábados se vían radiantes de felicidá, paseando por el pueblo, brazo con brazo, rumbo a Doña María, único restorán que había en el pueblo. Pero esa dicha duró muy poco, porque en cosa de unas cuatro semanas, desapareció de repente la Raquel, robándole a Casimiro el poco dinero que tenía en su casa, contoy muebles, trastes, ropa y todo. Volvió el pobre Casimiro de su trabajo en la plaza para encontrar su casa completamente vacía y en un silencio espantoso. Cómo sería de duro el choque de ver im afamao curandero como Casimiro que resultó gritando, echando espumarajos por la boca, en una chaqueta de locos, forcejeando con los enfermeros que se lo llevaron derechito al manicomio. Y de ahí en adelante, jamás quiso curar a las mujeres. "A Mesilla, váyanse a ver a la Felícitas," y cerraba la puerta imediatamente cuando le llevavan alguna pobre mujer muriéndose de tristeza, sufriendo un ataque de rabia.

Claro, como siempre hay chismes, dicían algunos de los que por allí andaban cortando la alfalfa, las vecinas que se asomaban, que la tal Raquelita era una de esas viejas sueltas. Yo les diré que esa mujercita a mí nunca me engañó. Que había tardes, cuando Casimiro estava en la plaza, que llegava un hombre joven de unos veinte años y se pasaba la tarde con ella. De eso no les podré dicir una palabra, como yo no lo vi. Pero sí les podré dicir que cuando Casimiro volvió del hospital, callao, adolorido, se le oía en las noches, en su casa oscura, tristemente tocando la guitarra y cantando la misma canción, vuelta y vuelta, que asegún algunos, era algo que le cantaba la mentada Raquel.

Adió, adió, querida
Non quero la vida
me la amargates tú.
Cuando tu maa' te parió y
te echó al mundo,
corazón ella non te dio
para amar un segundo
para amar un segundo.
Mas búscate otro amor
Allá detra'diotra puerta
Allá busca otro protetor
que para mí sos muerta,
que para mí sos muerta,
Adió, adió, querida
non quero la vida
me la amargates tú
me la quitates tú.

Dicían algunos que la mujercita esa le había enseñao muncho, hasta desas canciones que dizque son de de España o de lugares de por allá. De eso no sé nada, lo que sí sé es que se me llenaban los ojos de lágrimas cuando lo oía cantar en la oscuridá de su casita vacía. ¿Pero quién le mandó meterse en ese lío con esa niña? Yo no, eso sí que no, yo no lo hubiera hecho.

Sí, sí, ya sé que algunos dicen que to'o eso es puro cuento, puros chismes, que esa muchachita era nada más que la hija de doña Merceditas, de Antony, y que el loco del Casimiro perdio to'o su dinero y sus cosas en chanchuyas y negocios chuecos y que sacaba esas canciones de libros viejos, y lo demás que se dice, pero yo les estoy contando lo que a mí me contaron.

Bueno, como les iva diciendo, recién salido del hospital, Casimiro se vía, al principio, profundamente cansao, triste, metido en sus propios pensamientos, calladísimo, con ojos raros que vían al espacio como si tratara de encontrar alguna solución a algo que no tenía solución. Y poco a poco dejó de ir a su acostumbrao sitio en la plaza y se vía meditando en el desierto o en frente de su casa vacía, que por el resto de su vida dejó desamueblada. Nosotros lo ívamos a visitar, pobre hombre, y nos fijávamos que sus conversaciones empezavan a ser diferentes, a tomar otras diresiones. Mejor dicho, ya casi no hablava, nomás dicía lo que consideraba lo más importante. Sentao en un tapetito en el suelo, y nosotros también en el suelo, ya que no havía sías, ni nada en su casa y nos dicía que nunca havía podido olvidar el mundo de los muertos y que ahora quería, en vida, llegar a esa perfecta calma y serenidá que havía visto allá en ese mundo. Yo creo que sería verdá porque cuando curava a sus pacientes y hasta cuando hablava con nosotros, se repitía a sí mismo, "Todo pasa, todo cambia, no permitas que te turbe ni el vuelo de la mariposa, ni las tormentas de la tierra, ni el susurrar del viento ni los terremotos del alma, porque el centro del universo, que eres tú, y tú, y tú, y yo, está en perfecta paz y tranquilidá." El caso es que le empezaron a llegar más y más pacientes, del norte de Nuevo México, de Albuquerque, de Sierra Blanca, Tejas, y hasta de Juárez, cosa rara, porque ya saben ustedes que allá en México tienen de esos brujos y curanderos pero de a montón. Pos así como les digo, comenzó a ser muy conocido como consejero y médico, lo veíamos algunas veces en frente de su casita, sentao en la tierra, el paciente también, viéndolo intensamente, como si las palabras estuvieran sembrando algo en su alma el. No hay que negarlo, le fue bien en ese negocio, pero como les dicía antes, empezó Casimiro, no sólo a dícir cosas raras, sino también hacer cosas raras.

Fue entonces cuando le dio por hacer pinturas estrañas con colores raros como los que ves en un sueño y las puso por dondequiera en la casa. Bueno, digo estrañas, porque los que ívamos a visitarlo, de cuando en cuando, no entendíamos lo que víamos. "Son meditaciones y sueños," nos dicía y nosotros nos quedávamos en las mismas. Algunas de esas pinturas tenían cuatro montañas, una en cada lao, una arriba y una abajo con una vereda que suvía zig-zag, zig-zag, atravesando una lluvia de rayos, hasta llegar a lo alto, a una piedra relumbrante. "Es el cristal divino, el cuarzo," nos dicía, y abajo, un hombre viejo, flaco, con lentes, y solamente con un trapo blanco como zapeta, descalzo y desnudo, que suvía por la vereda como si tratara de llegar a la luz. "Es la visión del shamán que va a unirse a las fuerzas primarias de la creación." Y nosotros, "¿Ah, sí?" y nos quedávamos viendo la pintura sin entender nada, y lo escuchávamos sin entender nada tampoco. Cuando volvíamos a casa, to'os preocupaos nos dicíamos: "Entre más viejo, más loco. A la mejor allá en el hospital de los loquitos, allá donde lo mandaron, agarró todas esas maniyitas." Y ya sabrán que Casimiro empeoró con los años. ¿Que qué dicía? Bueno, parecía que dicía menos y menos, porque ya apenas hablava en conversaciones normales, con amigos y parientes, pero con los pacientes ponía mucha atención a esactamente lo que quería dicirles. A lo menos eso fue lo que me dijo Rogelio que sufrió una terrible depresión después de la muerte de Beto. Me dijo que asegún Casimiro, la palabra es sagrada y poderosa y que era la creación del cosmos, o del universo o algo así. Bueno, no se rían, eso es lo que me contaron a mí. Lo que sí les puedo dicir es que un día me dijo, "Si espresas con tu voz lo que vas hacer, has comenzao el pro-

ceso de la creación." Y ahora no sé por qué, pero cada vez
que me pongo a contarles la historia de Casimiro, me acuerdo
de eso.

Ya viejito Casimiro, empezaron los vecinos a notar que su
casita de adobe se venía derrumbando, pedazo a pedazo, contoy tablas, vigas y paderes. Vinieron los jóvenes a ofrecerle
componérsela, pero no, no quiso. Empezó entonces a mudarse
de cuarto en cuarto, asegún se caiban las paderes, hasta que
un día un relámpago como un zig-zag eléctrico, y luego un
trueno, tumbó por completo el techo y se quedó afuera, bajo
el cielo y el sol y las estrellas, su casita ahora hecha un montón de tierra y palos viejos ya blanquizos por el sol, por nues-
tros terribles vientos y el frío del desierto. "Bueno, hombre, y
qué ívamos hacer, si eso es lo que quería, no nos dejava acer-
carnos . . . viejito chiflao." Y fue cuando hizo algo inesper-
ado. Se puso unas sandalias viejas y así, viejito, too' tembe-
leque, desnudo con sólo un trapo blanco como un pañal, se
fue caminando, con un bordón, como pudo, y llegó a la casa
de Eduviges en Mesilla. Se asomó a la ventana y le dijo, "Ya
llegós tu momento. Tú que tienes esperencia en crear seres
nuevos, vente comigo porque tienes muncho que hacer." Y así
es cómo dicen que llegó Eduviges a ser la consejera-hierbera,
la adivinapoeta, partera, sobadora, y la mejor médica que jamás se ha visto en todas estas tierras, siendo que havía tantos
jóvenes que le pedían a Casi instrucción para ser brujos y curanderos. Pero no, fue la callada y tranquila Eduviges la que per-
fecionó la sabiduría de Casimiro, sus poemas y cuentos, sus
escritos donde anotaba los pasos de sus meditaciones, bueno,
así dicía: "pasos y escaleras," contoy los cuadros raros que les
descriví y montones de cuadernos donde diariamente com-
ponía cartas de amor, pos era todo lo que le pertenecía a Casi
en este mundo. Sí, es cierto que ha habido algunos que le han
dicho a Eduviges que haga algunos libros sobre sus propias
meditaciones o de sus poemas con los que cura a mujeres,
hombres y niños o sobre la magia de las hierbas o la energía
curitativa que tienen sus manos al sobar. Hasta le han dicho

que se comunique con un escritor mexicano como Juan José Arreola, creo que así es el nombre, para que le ayude a poner todo eso en escritos. Pero ya saben como es Eduviges: dice que las palabras havladas son las que verdaderamente valen y las que llegan directamente al corazón y al cuerpo. Algo así. Escribirá algún día todos sus conocimientos, de eso no hay duda, pero lo hará a su manera. En fin, vayan allá con doña Serafina para que oigan el cuento de Eduviges.

Bueno, como les dicía, un sábado en la mañanita del 6 de agosto, a la edá de 92 años, Casimiro Mendoza amaneció muerto, completamente desnudo, tirao en la tierra donde se había caido su casita. Parecía estar dormido y tan tranquilo se vía que hasta hubo quienes dijieron "¿Y qué si vuelve a resucitar? Tal vez no debemos enterrarlo tan pronto." A lo que contestó el Padre López, moviendo un poco la mano, como dándole la bendición, "No vaya a volver esta vez convertido en San José de Cupertino, patrón santo de los cohetes voladores, que según el Acta Sanctorum, fue el santo que más alto y más frecuentemente levitaba."

Pero no, que yo sepa, esta vez sí murió de a deveras Casimiro, pero a través de estas palabras, todas ciertas, les he dado a ustedes, a quienes me lo han pedido, y a los que me lo pidan en el futuro, el cuento de la vida de nuestro querido aunque estambólico, amigo. Y así fue y sigue siendo.

De la novela *Las Huellas de los Sueños*

Casimiro Mendoza, the Improvisor

Well then, since there are so many stories about the life of Don Casimiro, all wrong, of course, here I'm going to tell you the real true story of the aforementioned Casi who died recently, may he rest in peace. Well, you probably already

know that throughout his long life he enjoyed a special reputation; as a young man he was one heck of a good carpenter,
and he even got it into his head to become a saint carver.
Later on, he was one of our village's public scribes, and as a
mature man, he was our soothsayer, healer, and adviser to all
those who, fed up with life or sick in their soul, came to his
little house to seek relief from their troubles. Because of the
extraordinary and legendary things that happened to him,
some of the townspeople ascribed to him a disreputable noto-
riety. Some used to say—in fact, some still say—that he was a
liar, a phony, a fool, and all that, but others swear that he
was a first-rate healer, a spiritual and wise man, and the best
doctor that lived around these parts. Tall, thin, with long
arms and legs, a bit stooped, nearsighted, wearing small,
thick-lensed glasses, he looked like some sort of a strange bird
when, as a young man, he crossed the plaza with his long
strides, usually smoking and reading or staring right through
you with his glistening eyes, his thoughts somewhere else. Although he never married, everyone used to say that he was
always in love with one unmarried girl or another, or some
widow, and from time to time, he'd even risk his life by paying special attention to a good-looking married woman who
might go up to him in the plaza where he earned his living
writing letters, or who came to his house to request some of
his varied services.

　　Look, I had the occasion to hear some of the old men
tell how young Casimiro made beautiful pine furniture, all
carved with little birds and angels and hearts and flowers,
and who knows what else. And also perhaps because of some
spiritual rapture, or maybe because he simply needed the
money, he carved, by special request, saints like Saint Judas
Thaddeus, or if it was for women, images of Saint Barbara,
who they say was the first feminist saint in history, or something like that—I don't know how to say that word they use
nowadays. During those years when Casi was barely twenty-
five or so, he was making plans to get married, building him-

self a little brick house, carving lovely furniture for when he married Genoveva, a really beautiful girl—I happened to know her, she had a very unusual way of looking at you, a bit cross-eyed, she was, and everybody said it made her look a lot more sensual than she might have been otherwise. But that wedding never took place. Two days before the ceremony, with everything ready, the beautiful Genoveva dropped dead— some said that it was some sort of stroke—leaving poor Casi in the deepest depression and despair, like without hope. After the funeral he went to bed and spent six months nearly motionless, not wanting to do anything, only wanting to die—he told me that. He didn't even bother with the house he'd just built, or the furniture. He even stopped carpentering, and his parents had to sell off all the things he'd been working on so lovingly for so long, or give them away.

He must have wanted to die so much that he got his wish, or rather, that's what they say. In that depression he had an attack of meningitis, or however it's pronounced, and he went into a coma. His parents quickly took him to the General Hospital in El Paso, and they sent him by plane, unconscious, nearly dead, to San Antonio, and then, in another plane to Dallas and then to Houston where you find all those famous doctors who specialize in brains. All the doctors said there was nothing to be done, that he was going to die, and one of them even told the exact day and the exact time when Casi'd pass on to a better life. His grieved parents, who only a year earlier had buried their other son, Azaleo—I'm sure some of you remember that fine, young musician—had no other choice than to bring him back to the village, and the poor dying guy arrived in an ambulance, on a stretcher, no less, with all the neighbors looking on and feeling sorry. Well, they started getting ready for Casimiro's inevitable death; the priest arrived and gave him extreme unction and all that, and they began to prepare for the wake with all the rosaries at the ready and the announcements out, and they even asked some of his friends to write obituaries to read at the funeral. One of the most beautiful eulogies, it really moved you, was the one written by Don Salomón, the other carpenter, who to be honest, had never been too fond of his talented competitor, but in the obituary he talked with a lot of feeling, just as if it had come out of the Bible, all about Casi's work and the deep friendship that had united the two carpenters and saint carvers. His parents and the neighbor women laid Casimiro out and put him in one of the rooms in his parents' house right there on the plaza, and his friends went by in a line and looked at him lying there, with his body in full view, all long and bony and his eyes shut tight; he had, for all practical purposes, really left this world. The women crossed themselves and said, "It's Genoveva come for him, she took him with her, you remember how jealous she always was," and the men peeked in at the window and saw him there motionless and took their hats off in respect and looked down at their boots, although some of them did say, "He's pretending, we all know him, he's been pretending all this time."

Now I couldn't say that that was true, but early the morning of Saturday, August 6, at daybreak, exactly the date that the doctors had said that he was going to die, Casimiro opened his eyes, and looking sort of furious at all those sobbing women carrying rosaries, said "What the hell am I doing here again?" and the cynical ones said, "What did I tell you? He was trying to put another one on us." Well, anyway, up jumped Casimiro from his bed, which was surrounded by candles, perfectly alert and healthy, you can't imagine, and took a bath to get rid of all the powders and ointments and all that oily stuff that Felícitas had rubbed him with, and then sat down and ate this humongous plate of vermicelli and meat and chile, and then began to read his obituaries, laughing boisterously from time to time or smiling dryly at some point in his reading. Well, who knows what got into him after that, because they say that the following morning, he left his parents' house with this little table and an old typewriter and sat in the shade under some trees in the plaza to wait for clients to ask him to write letters in English or Spanish—he could do both—like letters to the federal government asking about some check that had gotten lost, or to the mayor of Las Cruces complaining about the awful medical services in the village, or to someone's relative in Mexico about somebody being sick or dying, say, an uncle or aunt or brother-in-law; he even asked for girls' hands in marriage like they used to in those days, you'll probably remember, not like now when all they say is we're getting married, and that's it, with no respect for the nice customs we used to have. What Casi liked most, though, was writing love letters, and that was what he did best of all.

When I was still a kid, I used to see Casi writing those famous love letters. I'd go to the plaza on Sunday mornings to speak to others waiting around for their wives to come out of mass, and talking about the terrible state of the irrigation ditches and the high cost of fertilizers and that sort of thing. Frequently, to have a few laughs, I'd go to the corner where Casi sat and always had a lot of customers gathered around waiting their turn, or just hanging around, because there's no two ways about it, when the fellow was inspired he'd really let go: he'd close his eyes with feeling and let his imagination run wild, reciting out loud and writing it all down at the same time, and of course, you got a real good show right there on the plaza. Casi, in those days, was a real eccentric, a real weird one, so to speak. Now don't you go thinking he just wrote straight away. Oh, no, he first questioned his clients for a long time to get all the details; his clients were nearly always men who wished to give their mistresses or girlfriends or fiancées or wives or what not a little poem or some written amorous declaration, something they wouldn't be caught dead doing in person.

Well, you can imagine, with young Casimiro's reputation, what sorts of things he asked the men, and, of course, what some of those cynical jokesters answered, because Casi wanted to know what color hair she had, what color her eyes were, and about her skin, and if she was tall or short, or if she had

wide, sensuous lips and long, silky eyelashes, a lovely long
neck and perfect feet, and any distinguishing mark like, say, a
dimple or a birthmark, and if so, where was it, and what did
she dream of. He even asked secret things that only the man
could know, like some passionate quirk that she had, and so
on and on, questions like that. What he always wanted to
know, though, was if she was a bit cross-eyed, and there was
always some guy who said yes. When that happened, boy
was he inspired! He was overcome with love, and he'd hit his
typewriter and let it rip, composing and reciting and writing
all at the same time. He always kept the carbon copy and
gave the other to the customer who signed his name or made
a little cross, and then Casi charged him a few dollars, and
that was the end of the business transaction.

At the other side of the plaza Don Secundino cursed and
swore. He'd been working for years as the town scribe, and he
saw how day after day, Casimiro got all the customers with
his flowery language and exaggerations and the show he put
on in public. Some of the women who got letters said they
were pure poetry, that they'd keep them forever, but there
were others who wouldn't let their husbands or boyfriends get
near Casi, you see, he got to know too much about their hidden secrets. Furthermore, they noticed that he started staring
at them, you know, with that special kind of look, at the post
office, at the shops, in church, as if he knew something very
personal about them, as if he was in love with them even.

His being a scribe started, as I said, as a direct result of his
strange experience in the world of the dead. Now another leg-
end was added to his fame, that he had died and resurrected.
So often did they ask him to tell them all he'd seen and who
he'd talked to when he was dead, that he ended up conduct-
ing special sessions, with an entry fee, of course, of one or
two dollars, and he'd tell them all about his experiences in
the world of the dead.

"Look here," he'd say, "the first thing I remember seeing is
this big shining light that wrapped me all up; it brought peace

and calm and made me go up, up, through some bright sun-
beams, up, up, to a high place where you could see four mountains, each at the four points of the universe. The way up led
to a brilliant white stone, and I saw a lot of people I knew up
there, and they all smiled very serenely and said hi, very happy,
and when I talked to them they seemed to know what was
going on down here in the village. I even saw my younger
brother Azaleo, but everyone else was Azaleo, too, because it
seemed that there wasn't any difference between one dead
person and another up there. I was looking for Genoveva, of
course, but all of the dead women were Genoveva, too. Well,
when I spoke to her, or rather, to one of the Genovevas, she
seemed so happy that it made me quite angry, since I've been
suffering so much for her, hour after hour, day after day, down
here. I told her how I felt, and she said, real calm, 'If you're
getting mad and jealous, that means you're not dead yet, so
go back down there to earth. And be sure you say hello to
Mama and Papa when you get down there.' I hardly had time
to tell her how grieved I've been because she's not with me,
and how I was going to dedicate the rest of my life writing
love letters to her, and that I'd always love her throughout
eternity, and that she should wait for me to join her so we
could be together properly, and she then said, very quietlike,
'Forget it, man. There's none of that sort of thing up here. Get
back to where your fate sends you'."

Anyway, these sessions were real strange because Casimiro
kept adding things and more and more details. As well as being a scribe and giving advice, a lot of people came to ask if
he'd seen whatsisname and whatsername up there, and if
they'd asked after them. Casimiro would always answer very
seriouslike, "Your mama's keeping track of all the damn fool
things you do when you get drunk on Saturday nights." And
the patient would ask, "And does it make her sad? Is she suffering on my account?" And Casi, looking right into his eyes,
would say, "It's you who're suffering. It's you who's sad with
the pain you've got inside. Get rid of it."

Some continued to think that Casimiro was a big liar and that the best thing to do was to take no notice of him since he was probably doing more harm than good in his sessions on death with the village boozers, and with the young kids who smoked pot and took drugs and so on, stuff that at my old age I've never used. Take the case of Benito, remember? He'd been a drunkard for years, just like San Benito, patron saint of the drunks, for whom he'd been named and who, like his saint, gave up drinking. "What did he do?" they asked Benito. "How did that old buffoon cure you?" And Benito would answer, "Well, he didn't give me no drugs like the doctors in Las Cruces and El Paso. He just cured me with words. He had me recite poems and stories and that's how he cured me." And they said, "No, man, you gotta be kidding; you don't cure somebody like that. He must have given you something." But Benito would say, "No, that's how it was. I still know all those poems, I learned them by heart. Casimiro had me repeat after him just as if he was looking for the same thing I was.

"My Lord, if I, with my limitations and with my human weaknesses forget Thee at times, Thou, oh Lord, do not forget me for one instant. Thou who are my creator, keep on loving me so I learn to love myself. Believe in me so I learn to believe in myself. Oh, my Creator who gave me life, help me to live."

"Now repeat it," Don Casimiro would say, "repeat it until the words reach the corners of your heart, until they are the very breath of your soul. Repeat it when you feel like going off to join your friends at the bar because that's when you're suffering the pains of your illness. And if you still feel like drinking, get close to the powers of creation and re-create yourself. Start sawing wood and making furniture or saints, build houses, write or sing songs. Create paintings with whatever's in your heart and soul, and every day write a love poem which is to get close to the origins of reproduction. And if your true purity doesn't bloom, then get hold of a tree and don't let go, since the tree is the sacred symbol of a new life."

And some of the neighbors, when they saw Benito crying and trembling from head to toe, holding onto a tree, would say, "Uuuu, that poor guy's nuttier now than his master." Anyway, that's how Benito described his treatment, and he always did say that what all those doctors with their diplomas and certificates on the walls of their offices were unable to do, Casi was able to do. Of course, I'm not saying that Casimiro was always successful, mind you, you've only to think of the recent case of Rigoberto, but, like they say, Beto didn't really want to create a new life for himself.

Up to this point, Casi would deal only with men in his healing business; he only cured men, that is, and he left the women to Felícitas. In fact, some used to say—you know that there are always gossip mongers around—that Casi and Felícitas way back when were seen praying and meditating together in the desert, and God only knows what else they did, too, and one even heard the rumor that Casi was the father of Feli's daughter, Eduviges. Now nobody ever really knew if that was definitely true or not. The truth is that Felícitas, the herbalist, midwife and layer-on of hands, and Casi, our public scribe, adviser, and healer were, in a certain way, competitors in the same business, so to speak, so some people refused to believe all those stories. Anyway, when Casi still attended to women, something really horrible happened, something really sad, and after that episode, he never let women into his house. Besides, that painful experience produced another change in his life, you might say.

Even though there are a lot of different versions of what happened, I know the exact truth because it was personally told to me this way: that one day this really pretty fifteen-year-old girl came into the plaza crying and sat down at Casi's side, who must have been about forty or so by then. Amid sobs and more sobs, tears and more tears, hiccups and more hiccups, and holding on to Casi's handkerchief, she told him how her husband had beaten her up, how he had abandoned her, how she didn't know what to do because she'd no money, and that she'd be better off dead. And Casimiro, completely stupefied by the beautiful dark-skinned girl with green eyes, curly hair down her back, didn't say anything at all because he didn't know what to say, but then, he pulled himself together a bit and started asking about her married life and cause and effect and all those things. After they'd talked several times in the plaza, this girl—Raquel she said was her name—and Casimiro became real good friends, and in a matter of a few days, Raquelita moved in with Casimiro, and on Saturdays you'd see them looking radiantly happy, walking through town arm in arm, heading for Doña María's, the only restaurant we had in town. But you couldn't call it long-lasting happiness, since it took only four weeks for Raquel to take off unexpectedly with all the money Casimiro had hidden about his house, not that it was much, along with all his furniture and clothes and everything. Poor Casimiro got home from work in the plaza, and there was the house, all empty and dreadfully quiet. You can imagine what a terrible shock that must have been to see a healer like Casi yelling and foaming at the mouth, in a strait jacket and wrestling with the nurses who tried to hold him down and who finally took him straight to the lunatic asylum. And from then on, he wouldn't have anything to do with women and their ailments. "Go to Mesilla, go see Felícitas," he'd say and shut the door whenever somebody brought him a poor woman dying of sorrow or suffering from an attack of fury.

And as you know, there's always gossip; some of the guys who were nearby cutting alfalfa, as well as women neighbors, said that Raquelita was one of those loose women. I have to admit that that strange little girl never fooled me, no sir, not for a minute. They used to say that in the afternoons when Casimiro was in the plaza, a young man about twenty used to come and spend hours with her. I can't say anything about that since I never saw him. But I can tell you that when Casimiro got out of the hospital, all quiet and hurt, you could hear him at night in his darkened house sadly playing the guitar and singing the same song over and over again, which some said was one of the many things that the aforementioned Raquel taught him.

Farewell, farewell, beloved,
In this life I no longer want to be,
Oh, how you've embittered it for me.
When your ma bore you,
And pushed you out into this world,
A heart she failed to give you
To love for even a second,
To love for even a second.
So look for another love
Behind some other door.
There look for another protector,
Since for me you exist no more,
Since for me you exist no more.
Farewell, farewell, beloved,
In this life I no longer want to be,
Oh, how you've embittered it for me,
Oh, how you've embittered it for me.

Some said he really learned a lot from her, that little girl, even those songs which they say come from Spain, or places like that, but I wouldn't know about those things. What I do know is that my eyes filled with tears every time I heard him singing in the darkness of his empty house. But who told him to get mixed up with a young girl like that? Not me. You wouldn't catch me doing a thing like that, no siree. Yes, yes, I know some say that all this is just a story, nothing but gossip, that that little girl was nobody else but doña Merceditas's daughter who lived in Anthony, and that nutty ol' Casimiro lost everything in crooked dealings and that he took all those songs from old books, and on and on, but I'm telling you the story I was told.

Well, anyway, as I was saying, when Casimiro got out of the hospital, you'd see him at first looking real tired and sad, all lost in his thoughts, very quietlike, staring into space as if he were trying to find an answer to something that didn't have one. And little by little, he stopped going to his place in the plaza, and you'd see him meditating in the desert or in front of his empty house which he never furnished again as long as he lived. We'd go visit him, poor guy, and we'd notice how his conversations weren't the same; they were going in other directions, you might say. To be more exact, he didn't really talk much anymore, he just said what was important, and that's all. Sitting on a little mat on the floor, with us sitting also on the floor, because as I told you, there weren't any chairs around or anything else, he would tell us that he'd never really been able to forget the land of the dead, and that he wanted, while still alive, to reach that perfect calm and serenity that he'd seen in that other world. I think he meant it, too, because when he would talk to his patients, and even when he was talking to us, he used to say to himself, "All passes, all changes, let nothing disturb you, not the flight of the butterfly nor the storms of the earth, not the whispering of the wind nor the earthquakes of the soul because the center of the universe which is you and you and you and me is always in perfect peace and tranquility." The fact is that more and more people started coming to consult him, from northern New Mexico, from Albuquerque, from Sierra Blanca, Texas, and even from Juárez, which was odd, because in Mexico, as you know, they've got healers and sorcerers coming out their ears. Well, just as I've said, he began to grow very famous as an adviser and healer and we'd see him in front of his little house sitting on the ground with a patient looking at Casi very intenselike, as if the words were planting seeds in the depths of his soul. No two ways about it, his business certainly prospered, but as I said before, Casimiro didn't just say strange things, he did them, too.

That was when he started painting those odd pictures with weird colors like you see in dreams sometimes, and he put those paintings all over his house; I say they were strange, because when we went to see him from time to time, we didn't know what we were looking at. "They're meditations," he'd tell us, "that's what they are." And we were still in the dark as to what they were. Some of them showed four mountains, one at each side, one up, one down, with a path that zigzagged across a rain of lightning until it reached the top where this shining stone was. "That's the divine quartz crystal," he would say, and down below was this thin old man with glasses on, and only a white loincloth and no shoes, all naked, going up the pathway, as if trying to get to the light. "That's the shaman's dream, and he's going to join the primary forces of creation," he said. And we'd say, "Oh yeah?" And we'd stare at the picture and still didn't understand anything. On the way home, all worried, we would say to each other, "The older he gets, the crazier he gets, no doubt about that. Maybe he picked up those crazy ideas when they locked him up with the other loonies." And as you know, he got worse as he got older, you all know that. What did he say? Well, it seems he didn't say much, he said less and less. In fact, he hardly talked at all anymore with friends and relatives, but he paid very special attention when he spoke to those who came to consult him; he knew exactly what he wanted to tell them. At least that's what Rogelio told me when he had this terrible depression that came upon him when his best friend Beto died. He said that according to Casimiro, the word is sacred and powerful and that the word is the creation of the cosmos or the universe, or something like that. Well, don't laugh, that's what Rogelio told me. What Casi did say to me one day though was, "If you say aloud what you are going to do, you've begun the process of creation." And I dunno why, but every time I start to tell the story of Casimiro, I remember that.

When Casimiro was real old, the neighbors started noticing that his little house was starting to collapse, adobe by adobe, along with the boards and beams and walls. The young folk came and offered to rebuild it for him, but, no, he didn't want that. It was then that he started moving from one room to another as the walls fell, until one day a flash of lightning like an electric zigzag, then a thunderbolt, and the roof fell in, leaving him outside under the sky, the sun, and the stars, his house just a heap of rubble, earth and old sticks that bleached in the sun with the awful wind we have here and the cold of the desert. Well, man, and what were we to do, if that's the way he wanted it. He wouldn't let us come near, nutty old coot. And that was when he really did something nobody expected. He put on some old sandals and all weak and trembling, the old man, naked with his white cloth like a diaper, went walking with his pilgrim's staff to Eduviges's house in Mesilla. He went up to her window and said, "Your moment has arrived. You, who have the experience of creating new living beings, come with me, you have much to do." And that's how they say Eduviges became the adviserherbalist, the diviner-poet, midwife, layer-on of hands, and the best doctor that has ever been known in all of these lands, even though there are so many young men who have asked Casi for instruction, wanting to become sorcerers and healers. But no, it was the quiet and serene Eduviges who perfected Casimiro's wisdom, his poems and stories, and the writings in which he jotted down the steps of his meditations. Well, that's what he called them, "steps and ladders," along with those weird pictures I mentioned, and piles of notebooks in which he daily composed love letters. And that was everything that had belonged to Casimiro. Yes, it's true that some people have told Eduviges to write books about her own meditations and her poems with which she cures women, men, and children or about the magic power of plants or the heal-ing energy of her hands. They've even told her to get in touch with a Mexican writer like Juan José Arreola, I think that's his name, so he'll help her put all that in books. But you know how Eduviges is: she says that the spoken words are what really are important and are the ones that go straight to the heart and body. Something like that. Someday she'll write down all her wisdom, there's no doubt about that, but she's going to do it her way. Well, if you want to hear the story of Eduviges, go one of these days to see doña Serafina.

Well, anyway, one early Saturday morning, August 6, when he was ninety-two years old, Casimiro Mendoza woke up dead, completely naked, without a stitch on, flat out on the ground where his house had collapsed. He seemed to be sleep-ing, and he looked so peaceful that there were even some who said, "And what if he resurrects again? Maybe we'd better not be in a hurry to bury him." But Padre López, waving his hand a bit, as if giving him the benediction, said, "Well, let's hope he doesn't come back this time as San José de Cupertino, the patron saint of rockets, who according to the Acta Sancto-rum, was the saint who most frequently levitated and who went higher than anybody else."

But, no, as far as I know, that time Casimiro really did die, but by means of these words, every one true, I assure you, I've given you and to all those who might ask in the future, the story of our beloved although eccentric friend. And that's the way it is, and ever shall be.

From the novel *Las huellas de los sueños (The Footprints of Dreams)*. Trans-lation by Alita Kelley with suggestions by Rowena A. Rivera.

MARGARITA TAVERA RIVERA

Sed

*Sigilosamente, escurrióse por entre los arbustos, de reojo, lo vi,
presentí que se lanzaba hacia mí* . . . Los primeros síntomas
imitan los de un resfriado común; un malestar general, perío-
dos de alta fiebre, seguidos de escalorios que hacen tronar los
dientes, náusea. Es una náusea agobiante que provoca asco
hacia todo; hacia el anhelado aroma del café de la manaña,
el aroma penetrante del pan recién horneado, estos olores,
antes un deleite del olfato, son una molestia más para la garganta ya irritada, que sangra ligeramente cada vez que la
náusea induce el vómito, un vómito seco, que deja a la persona fatigada, intensificando así el sentido de malestar que in-
vade al enfermo. Este malestar quita el sueño, y al descansar
sólo se logra dormitar, y es durante este estado entre medio
despierto, medio dormido que suceden los sueños fantásticos.

En los sueños aparecen perros, unas veces muchos, otras
veces uno solo. Era este perro, el solitario, el que me seguía,
intentaba morderme, entonces él corría y yo corría, y siempre
me preguntaba cómo era que yo podía correr tanto. Cuando
ya no podía ni dar un paso más, siempre despertaba. Y en un
rincón de mi mente, agazapada, la pregunta clave. ¿y el día
que no despierte a tiempo, qué?

*Sentí sus colmillos, rasgaron mi vestido, la media, el
muslo* . . . La infección al sistema nervioso se desarrolla rápidamente, si el desafortunado no se atiende a los once días
después de infectado, muere. Implacable sigue su desarrollo
natural, el malestar general se vuelve más abrumador. Los
primeros síntomas se agudecen. La producción de saliva au-

menta, y en conjunto la incapacidad para controlarla, la in-
habilidad para tragar lo lleva a uno de regreso al babeo infan-
til, ya que la irritación de la garganta se agravia al intentar
tragarse el exceso producido por la glándula salival. La saliva
se escapa por las comisuras de los labios y corre, los hilillos
serpentiando por el cuello, salpicando la ropa, mientras la
mano sostiene el pañuelo empapado en el regazo. Los cambios bruscos de temperatura provocan reacciones extremas ya
que la piel ha desarrollado una extremada sensibilidad al calor y al frío, que hacen que el paciente titirité de frío cubrién-
dose con mantas pesadas para al minuto tirarlas por el suelo
al reaccionar extremadamente a cualquier calorcito. Se agu-
dizan también los sentidos de la vista y del oído. Debe buscar
un lugar apartado, en penumbra donde no llegue la luz, donde
el sol no logre penetrar, ya que la luz le lastima los ojos, y los
aleteos de la cautiva mariposa nocturna le destrozan los oídos
y el crujir de las paredes le taladra las sienes suavemente. Es
durante esta fase de la enfermedad cuando cualquier cambio
brusco puede causar una reacción violenta en el individuo ex-
hibiendo un comportamiento completamente fuera de lo nor-
mal que se da sin ninguna motivación.

Los perros fantásticos de los sueños de las madrugadas tienen alas y vuelan, aunque hasta sin ellas corren tan veloces
que parecen no pisar la tierra. Semejan los recursos cinemato-
gráficos del "slow motion" que suspenden la acción o pasan
tan lentamente en el aire como cualquier chuparrosa. En los
sueños los perros son mansos, fieles, bondadosos encarnando
el perro mitológico, el mejor amigo del hombre.

Levanté el brazo, cubriéndome el rostro, grité, mi espalda
contra el barandal frío, metálico . . . En un sueño anterior, uno
de tantos, siempre me seguía un perro, un perro aparente-
mente manso, se acercaba, postrándose a mis pies, intentaba
engreírse conmigo; yo lo ignoraba; pero al darle la espalda se
agitaba, se enfurecía ante mi menosprecio y me ladraba, per-
siguiéndome. Yo corría, olvidando los consejos antiguos—No
le muestres miedo, si corres te alcanza y te muerde—pero la

lógica y el pánico están en diferentes esferas de nuestro cerebro y no hay cruce de información, entonces yo corría y él me seguía, cruzábamos calles, atravezábamos bosques, íbamos por entre los ríos, nunca puedo explicarme cómo corríamos tanto, el perro y yo.

Se volvió, regresó a su sitio al escuchar la orden de su amo—Ven, échate Chango . . . El fin se acerca, se dejan sentir los ataques, que le dan el nombre a la enfermedad; hidrofobia, que significa aversión al agua. Al ver el agua, al oirla o al visualizarla en cualquiera de sus formas induce en el afectado la constricción de la garganta, se pierde el control de las extremidades corporales, las facciones faciales se contorcionan y queda en el lugar del ser humano algo que se revuelca en el suelo, dejando huellas como los caracoles, con la cara desfigurada e incapaz de controlar los más sencillos movimientos de su cuerpo.

Ya solamente queda la espera, la muerte inevitable se anuncia en la parálisis que se apodera lentamente del cuerpo del infectado. La parálisis empieza en las piernas, los brazos, siguen luego los sistemas centrales, los que mantiene el cuerpo con vida. Deja de latir el corazón, los pulmones dejan de respirar, la sangre se estanca en las venas al dejar de funcionar el corazón y llega al final el descanso, la muerte deseada que le recupera la dignidad humana al ser atormentado.

El otro sueño era de muerte, muerte de perro. Encontrar un perro rabioso era así como un día de circo. La noticia se difundía por todo el pueblo. La voz corría, allá por la esquina de Jackson y Bandera anda un perro rabioso, y todos se congregaban, unos con piedras, otros con ramas secas o pedazos de madera, lo que fuera para matar el perro antes que fuera a morder a algún cristiano porque matar a una mujer u hombre rabioso no es tan fácil como matar un perro.

Al oeste del freeway, en el barrio de Guadalupe sucedió. Un barrio lleno de niños jugando en las calles faltas de asfalto, sin banquetas donde el murmullo por las tardes era de chicharras y de conversaciones amenas. En uno de estos barrios pasó. Y le pasó a don Chema. Don Chema era un hombre de por aquí, sin familia, que comía donde le daban y dormía donde podía. Era conocido de todos y pariente de nadie. Y una noche al dormir sobre su costal de jute, acurrucado bajo su cobija roja, en la esquina de la iglesia, allí donde se resguardaba del frío y de la lluvia bajo el aguacate frondoso, lo encontró el perro. Desde entonces se volvieron inseparables. Eran viejos amigos, acompañaba a don Chema en sus vueltas por el pueblo. Lo acompañaba a su trabajo, al parque a tomar el sol. Los dos se pasaban las mañanas allí, Don Chema dormitando en un banco y el perro roncando a sus pies. El perro era negro con una mancha blanca en la cara y sus cuatro calcetas. Le decían "El pantalón." Siempre saludaba a don Chema, moviendo la cola, corriendo de aquí a allá hasta que don Chema le tiraba cualquier cosa. Entonces "El pantalón" corría, levantaba lo que don Chema le había tirado, regresaba y se lo entregaba a don Chema como si fuera un gran tesoro. Luego empezaban su peregrinación diaria.

Inesperadamente desapareció "El pantalón" por varios días. Cuando no llegó por la noche don Chema se preocupó, pero sabía que el perro algunas veces se distraía, pero siempre regresaba. El día siguiente no llegó y don Chema empezó a indagar. Alguien lo había visto el día anterior allá por el centro, derrumbando unos botes de basura, otro lo había visto cerca de la estación del Greyhound levantando la pata sobre las llantas de los autobuses galgos. Don Chema dejó de preocuparse, llegaría esa noche. Pero no llegó esa noche, ni la siguiente. Finalmente apareció como una semana más tarde. Llegó a la esquina de la iglesia donde don Chema se preparaba para pasar la noche. Esa noche fue diferente, "El pantalón" llegó de mal humor, se enfureció cuando don Chema trató de taparlo con su cobija. "El pantalón" a duras penas podía arrastrase en sus cuatro patas, cosa que pasó inadvertida por don Chema, pues estaba más dormido que despierto. Cuando don Chema le pasó la mano por el espinazo, para calmarlo, "El pantalón" se volvió enfurecido y le mordió la mano.

Don Chema no se lo dijo a nadie, pero "El pantalón" amaneció tieso por la mañana. Al encontrar a don Chema llorando su perro los vecinos indagaron la razón de su muerte. Don Chema planteó su ignorancia de las causas, se oyó decir que había muerto de rabia, ya que no traía heridas de ninguna clase, don Chema se encogió de hombros. Al ver a don Chema con la mano envuelta en una manta sucia, llegaron a la conclusión que lo había mordido el perro. Todos sabían que dos huérfanos se buscaban, que dormían juntos allí en la esquina de la iglesia. Fue una decisión muy difícil, aunque no lo mataron como a un perro rabioso, sí vieron que murió como su perro. Aunque no hay una vacuna contra la enfermedad si hay un tratamiento, una serie de inyecciones dolorosas en el ombligo. Pero fue demasiado tarde para don Chema, ya habían pasado los once días.

Bajé la mano y palpé ligeramente donde el perro había puesto su hocico, sentí la sangre pegajosa . . . Anoche los perros me persiguieron. Eran dos, parecían hermanos; grandes, de la misma clase, del mismo tamaño, uno café el otro negro. Los vi venir desde lejos, corrían como venados, yo los veía acercarse, sin poder levantar los pies, se acercaban más y más, y yo gritaba, pero no oía mis gritos, solo veía la mueca del grito. Ya estaban encima de mí, se lanzaron, cerré los ojos y grité.

Thirst

Secretly, he slipped out from between the bushes. I saw him out of the corner of my eye and had a foreboding that he would jump on me. . . . . The first symptoms are like those of a common cold; general discomfort, periods of high fever followed by shivering, teeth chattering, and nausea. The nausea is oppressive; the patient experiences acute disgust at everything: the enticing smell of coffee in the morning, the penetrating odor of freshly baked bread—smells that normally give such pleasure now only further irritate the throat, which bleeds slightly each time the patient vomits, or attempts to vomit, with dry heaves that leave the person worn out, intensifying the general discomfort, so that the patient cannot sleep, can only doze. It is during this half-waking sleep that fantastic dreams occur.

Dogs appear in my dreams, sometimes many, sometimes only one. There was a dog, a lone dog that followed me and tried to bite me; then he would run and I too would run, always wondering how I could run so much. When I could go no further, I always awoke. In a corner of my mind there crouched the key question: if there comes a day when I don't wake up in time, what will happen?

I felt his fangs tearing my dress, my stocking, my thigh. . . . The infection which attacks the nervous system progresses rapidly, and if the patient is not treated within eleven days of being infected, death is unavoidable. The illness follows its implacable course; the general discomfort becomes overwhelming. Early symptoms become more acute. Salivation increases, together with the incapacity to control it; the patient regresses to a state of infantile dribbling from the mouth, since swallowing is no longer possible, with the irritation in the throat growing worse if any attempt is made to swallow the excess saliva. Saliva runs down the corners of the mouth, in threads down the neck, splashing the clothes of the patient in whose lap a soaked handkerchief is held. Sharp changes in temperature cause extreme reactions, and the skin has now developed an acute sensitivity to heat and cold, making the patient shiver and cover up with heavy blankets one moment, only to throw them on the floor a moment later in reaction to what appears to be intense heat. The senses of sight and sound become heightened. The patient must withdraw to a place in the shade, since light, especially sunlight, now hurts the eyes; the fluttering of a moth threatens to burst the eardrums; the creaking in the walls is like a soft drilling to the temples. It is during this stage of the illness that any brusque change can cause a violent reaction in the patient, whose behavior becomes totally abnormal without apparent motivation.

The fantastic dogs of my morning dreams have wings and fly, though sometimes they simply run so fast they seem not to touch the ground. They are like a slow-motion film where action is held in suspense, or run so slowly that they seem to hover in the air like a hummingbird. In my dreams the dogs are gentle, faithful, and kind, the incarnation of the mythological man's-best-friend.

I raised my arm, covering my face, and screamed, my back against the cold, metal rail. . . . In an earlier dream, one of many, there was always a dog following me, apparently a gentle dog, which came close and lay at my feet, trying to get me to pet it; I paid no attention, and when I turned my back, it became angered because I had treated it with contempt, and barked at me and began to chase me. I ran, forgetting sage or common-sense advice—never show them you're afraid; if you run they'll run after you and bite you—logic and panic inhabit different spheres of the brain, the information never crossed. I ran, and it ran after me; we ran across streets, through woods, between rivers; I could never explain to myself how we managed to run so much, the dog and I.

He turned and went back where he came from on hearing his master's voice: "Come, lie down Chango. . . ." The end is near, the attacks that have given the illness its name, "hydrophobia," or "aversion to water," begin to take place. If the patient sees, hears, or even imagines liquid in any form, the throat constricts; all control of the arms and legs is lost, and the facial features contort. Instead of a human being, the patient becomes an object writhing on the ground, incapable of controlling the least body movement, the distorted face leaving a trail of slime like a snail.

It is only a matter now of waiting for the inevitable end announced by a creeping paralysis which takes over the patient's body. Beginning with the legs and arms, this proceeds along the central nervous system which keeps the body alive.

The heart stops beating, the lungs stop flexing, blood no longer runs though the veins when the heart stops functioning, and finally rest comes with the longed-for death that restores human dignity to the tortured being.

The other dream was of death, a dog's death. Finding a mad dog used to be like going to the circus. Word spread all through the town. You heard there was a mad dog on the corner of Jackson and Bandera, and everybody gathered, some with stones, some with dry branches, some with pieces of wood, anything that would kill the dog before it bit some Christian soul; killing a man or a woman with rabies isn't as easy as killing a dog.

It happened to the west of the freeway in the section called Guadalupe. It was a barrio filled with kids who played on the unsurfaced streets, without sidewalks, where one could listen to the chirp of the cicadas or the hum of pleasant conversation in the evenings. It happened in one of those barrios. And it happened to don Chema. Don Chema was a man from around there; he had no family, he ate where they fed him, and he slept where he could. Everyone knew him; he was no one's relation. One night when he went to sleep on his sack, huddled under a red blanket near the corner of the church, shielded from the cold and rain under a leafy avocado tree, the dog found him. From that moment on they were inseparable. They grew to be old friends. The dog always accompanied don Chema around the town. It went to work with him, to the park to take sun. The two spent their mornings there, don Chema dozing on a bench and the dog snoring at his feet. It was a black dog with a white spot in its face and four white socks. They called it Pantalón. Pantalón always wagged his tail to greet don Chema and ran back and forth until don Chema threw something for him. Then Pantalón would run off and bring back the thing don Chema had thrown for him and give it to don Chema as if it were a great treasure. Then they'd start on their daily rounds.

Pantalón disappeared unexpectedly for several days. When

he didn't come back at night don Chema grew worried, but he knew the dog wandered off sometimes and always came back. The next day don Chema began making inquiries. Somebody had seen him the day before near the center of town knocking over trash cans; somebody else had seen him near the Greyhound station lifting his leg against the Greyhound bus tires. Don Chema stopped worrying; he'd come back at night. But he didn't come back that night nor the next. He finally showed up a week later. He arrived at the corner of the church where don Chema was getting ready to spend the night. That night was different. Pantalón had come back in a bad mood; he grew angry when don Chema tried to cover him with his blanket. Pantalón could barely drag himself along on his four feet, but don Chema didn't see this, for he was more asleep than awake by then. When don Chema ran his hand along Pantalón's back to calm him down, the dog grew angry and bit him. Don Chema didn't tell anyone, but next morning Pantalón was quite stiff.

When the neighbors found don Chema crying because his dog had died, they began to ask why. Don Chema said he had no idea and word got around it had rabies, since it had not been injured in any way; don Chema just shrugged. When they saw don Chema's hand wrapped in a dirty rag, they came to the conclusion the dog had bitten him. Everybody knew the two lost souls who slept there near the corner of the church had sought each other. It was hard to know what to do. They didn't just kill him like a mad dog, but they did see him die like his own dog had died. Although there isn't a vaccine against the illness yet, there's a way to treat it, a series of painful injections in the navel. But it was too late for don Chema, more than eleven days had gone by.

I lowered my hand and felt lightly where the dog had put his mouth. I felt the blood, sticky. . . . The dogs chased me last night. There were two, they seemed to be brothers; big ones, the same breed, the same size, one brown, the other black. I saw them coming from far off, running like deer. I saw them getting closer, and I couldn't move my feet. They were getting closer and closer, and I screamed, but I couldn't hear my screams. I could only see the silent grimace of the scream. They were upon me, they jumped, I closed my eyes and screamed.

Translation by Alita Kelley

EMILIA PAREDES

LA ERMITA (THE HERMITAGE)—EL CEDRO, GOMERA

A woman with white and silver hair
nestles in the deepest curve
of this forest floor. She is the mist
when she stirs
and loves that way of
the other woman
who welcomes her here. The forest
is her confidante. They sleep together
in the mystery of what it is
to be so beautiful and forgotten.
What they dream
enchants this night and I
hear their breathing as my own.
I have wandered here to kneel
beside the stream of their sadnesses
wet my mouth
and drink like a sister.
They offer me watercress
and I taste their delicate sweetness
like my own.
Tonight there are no words
but our thoughts
create this pleasure
as we speak together

in the gestures of the tree limbs
and her hair softly
softly sweeping our faces.

A PRISONER'S VIEW OF THE SKY

  for Phyllis Nauts

I am captive in my body.
People come in and out of me
with their anger and torments.
It bruises and bleeds.
Most days I have lain
flat on my back *pressing*
into the earth *away*
from fist and blade.
You are somewhere
I cannot see.
But today I find
I am fortunate
to be bound within my body
because the air rushing
out of me in mad laughter
forces my eyes open
when I least expect it, there
beyond the flutter of my eyelids:
the primary color of self
the blue of a gentle god
in a savage hour.
My body bruised and broken
but with eyes to see this sky
ineluctably blue.

When the peace
of this most sacred blue
finds its way into your prayers
I will be seeing it too.

Because of my body
I know
love also is blue
not flawlessly so, but apparent
in its absences, sometimes more sacred
than any stretch of sky I have ever seen.

GATHERING THE WILD FIGS—VIZCAINA, GOMERA

They are plump
and deeply purple.
Hungry and hot
we gorge ourselves
on their rich, red sweetnesses
that break into our mouths
like last and urgent kisses.
They are how this island rewards
our loving her so well
our venturing into the ache
of all her beauty
and abiding the gaze
of her myriad faces
with our myriad faces.
She was broken
but pieced herself together again
from the shards of the lava flow
from the destruction

she grew beautiful and strong.
Today we have paid the price
for her unveiling.
We have seen her scars
and she is not pleased
but ay
how she wanted us to see.
Ay, how we have hungered and thirsted to see.
And here her bounty.
We will taste her wild figs forever.
When we are old
our breaths will be scented with her wildness.
When we die we will know where we go.

FROM THE CLIFFS LEAPING—GUADA, GOMERA

I am longing to fly.
The sky so blue
like a mother's ache.
I never look down.
My eyes search for one
they have yet to see.
Faraway, I hear
the savage joy
of the canaries
so much more
than their tiny bodies
could ever hold.
I feel their song
fill my throat
up through the gully

and thick laurisilva.
And I know
my heart is near.

I am always surprised
to feel my body plummeting
while my spirit is soaring.
I never feel
the edge of rock or boulder
trying to convince my body
it has no alternatives.
I learn each time
longing is a way to be alive.

FROM THE MOUTH OF THE CAVE—GUADA, GOMERA

my heartbeat echoes.
In my subterranean pools
the laurel reaches for
and finds its life.
Water pours from my brow
and these cliffs stain
amber and green
with my effluence.

You have wandered
long and far
but have no fear.
I will gather the shell
of your body
into the deepest part of me
like the laurel
you will take root.

Soon canaries with wild songs
will nest in your branches.

I have not known a beginning
and you will not know an end.

EAGLE IN A SMALL SHADOW

I wake up with an urgency
not my own.
Something animal lives in me
without reason or hesitation
I am forced to breathe and want.
I am held by my neck and hair
forced to face the small
but formidable heap
a skinny, dark-eyed child
backed into the shadows
but with hands
reaching, please
naming her want with those hands
small, cold, but with fingers
fierce like talons
for some light.
I know
if I would reach my hand to hers she would snatch me
into her want
and I would scream
from the sinews of her flesh
no, and *no*
and I would be meaning
let me live.

ARLENE MESTAS

Mi Madrina

"Mi Madrina" was her title. Actually, she was my maternal grandfather's stepmother. She died in Albuquerque at her daughter's home. She was in her early nineties. The family was poor and did not have the means to have her transported by hearse from Gabaldón's mortuary in Albuquerque to El Rito. So an uncle volunteered to bring her in the back of his station wagon. I went to the mass with Aunt Rebecca and my maternal grandmother, or Grammita as we called her.

After mass, Grammita and I walked out behind the immediate family. This was the mid-sixties. Grammita pointed to the hippies who had sat at the back of the church. Hippies had nearly overrun El Rito. She said to me, "*Los greñudos vienen no más a comer.*" Hippies, by now, knew that a large meal ordinarily followed the burial and that no one was turned away.

A good-sized crowd gathered around the coffin for the final prayers before it was lowered into the ground. Someone brought out old nylon cords which had come wrapped around the coffin of a dead son who had died in Europe during World War II. These nylon cords were twenty-five to twenty-eight years old and were to be used again at today's burial. Men struggled to place the nylon cords under the gray cardboard coffin that clearly looked like cheap imitation marble. Four men took hold of the nylon cords in this do-it-yourself burial. They began to lower the coffin slowly, when one of the cords broke. The other cord held the coffin suspended at a precarious angle.

One of mi Madrina's daughters screamed, nearly fainted, and narrowly missed falling into the grave. Aunt Rebecca had her mouth covered with a white handkerchief. I looked at the surreal scene. A thin bony leg had pierced a hole in the coffin. The nylon hose on the leg dangled loosely.

Two men jumped into the grave and repaired the cord. One of the men pushed the leg back inside. The coffin was opened. Mi Madrina was dressed in pink and her face had been tinted to match the dress. At ninety-some she was a youthful blushing pink. The body was pulled back into place as if it were a doll that had slid in its package. The coffin was closed and then lowered. I walked away from the crowd at the gravesite. When I stood safely away from everyone, I let loose the suppressed hysterical sounds that had nearly escaped when I saw the bony leg shoot out of the cardboard box that held the tiny body. I looked at the clear blue sky, the sun dazzling white.

How Pancho Was Nearly Late to His Own Funeral

Pancho, my dad, was always late. He would not and could not be hurried. His tardiness was legendary. On Sundays, he would look after his animals, talk to God about the weather, and then he showered at the hour Mass began.

Midway through the sermon we would enter church. Late again to Mass, late to meetings. And even late when he read the hours of the S.A.T. as eight to twelve. He probably thought it was a social of some kind, but my brother was not allowed to take the test, as much as my dad argued with the test director. He took me to my wedding about half an hour late. My husband-to-be's family was pacing outside the church, probably thinking that their son was about to marry an unreliable woman. But I felt that my dad was trying to hang onto me as long as possible. The summer sky looked like "View Over Toledo" that evening when my dad refused to rush me to church. And even the local butcher told stories on my dad. He said that they often waited to watch my dad drive up with a steer to be butchered just as they were closing up for the night. Apparently, he had done it often enough that they knew my dad could not be hurried.

"You will be late to your own funeral," my mother often railed at him. She often started the car to warm it up before driving to Mass. She sat in the car ten to fifteen minutes before my dad finished showering. He'd walk out, grinning, his green eyes twinkling, and wearing his Stetson—his rancher's trademark.

When my dad died on July 3, one of my sisters was in Spain and one brother was in California on vacation. I was getting ready for a camping trip and family reunion. My daughters had already gone ahead with other family members to El Rito Canyon. I had just spent the weekend with him and mom. He had been hospitalized because he was not feeling well. But when he was released, he'd been given medication to speed the blood flow. He felt young again, he said. But after trying to close a barn gate, he'd gotten very tired and impatient. "My cowboy days are over," he said to me as he sat on the sofa. "I get tired too fast." "But dad, you're just out of the hospital— really you shouldn't even be out there. You know I can feed the calves." My mother's anxiety kept her in the kitchen. She knew what none of us would admit. She was fearful of being left alone with Dad. We all knew my dad was dying, but none of us would give voice to this horrible thought except my mother. I heard voices warning me that Dad would die soon. As I hugged my sister bound for Spain, a sole thought came to me loudly—"Do you want us to call you if Dad dies?" The gloomy thought hung over me as I waved good-bye to her.

She rushed back to hug Dad and later she said, "He looked at me as if he were looking at me for the last time, and I just had to come back to give him one last hug."

My brother who was in California had postponed his trip three or four times—and now that my dad had died, we didn't know where to reach him. When I was at the ranch that last weekend, I had wanted to yell at my brother to get home, that dad was sick, but of course, I couldn't say that—we were all gathered around the phone to make small talk with my brother. My dad sat there listening to me and my mother, monitoring the conspiracy of silence regarding his condition.

And so he died with my mother, his youngest daughter, and younger son in attendance. My mother called me very early on the third, saying that Dad really was very sick and that I should hurry if I wanted to see him alive. I thought it was just nerves on my mother's part. She frightened easily. And I had just seen him two days ago. My younger sister called to say that he had had a very mild heart attack but was feeling well—almost good enough to go to the reunion. Hadn't he gotten out of the hospital just a few days ago and gone to someone's fiftieth wedding anniversary? He was trying to pack as much living in as possible before he left.

Just as at a birthing, the calls from Vince, my brother-in-law, came faster and faster. "Your dad's really sick." "There's no hurry now." My phone bill recorded the collect calls that came in rapid succession.

I arrived in Alamosa early in the evening after picking up my daughters. Family members sat around and talked about my dad and waited for other family members to arrive. My sister-in-law, Vicki, walked in in tears. "Go see Johnny," she told me. "He needs you." He and I were the youngest and oldest—the bookends. My brother who had been with my dad when he died now refused to accept that my dad was gone. As he and his wife had driven up, he pointed to the light in the corrals, and said—"Dad's waiting for me. I've got to go help him." He refused to come into the house and wanted to go into the corrals where Dad waited for him to come help. I took Johnny by the arm and coaxed him into the house. He continued to want to go to the corrals but didn't make a move to go out. Vicki called her doctor, and she gave him two valiums and put him to bed. The next day he remembered not wanting to come into the house. But there are many people who have witnessed a dead one taking their leave. It is possible that Johnny did see Dad in the corrals. Now I wish that I had gone to the corrals with Johnny.

Earlier that evening, we called the tour that Judi was with in Spain, and they told us that she had gone to Morocco and would be back in three days. Vicki's sister lives in Spain and we called her—she was expecting Judi the next day. Judi called the following night about 2:00 A.M. "Please don't bury him until I get home. I have to see him." So we agreed to wait to bury him.

In the meantime, my brother moseyed home and stopped at an aunt's in Farmington before hearing of Dad. The family was at the mortuary the evening of the fourth, to see my dad, when my brother arrived driving at mata caballo speed. Patsy, his wife, was white from the terrifying drive. Their children were crying. My brother lived on the ranch with my parents, and his children were very close to their grandparents.

Judi had a terrible time making connections from Spain. She flew to Madrid where she sat in the plane for five hours waiting for the fog to lift. She missed a connecting flight from New York to St. Louis, and in St. Louis she missed another flight and had to spend the night. In the meantime, we had a rosary in Manassa, prayed by the Hermanos. Then we had another rosary in Alamosa the following night. We had the funeral Mass in Alamosa and the dinner in Manassa. My dad went back to the mortuary where he spent the weekend.

Judi finally arrived in Albuquerque and I picked her up. Finally, my dad was laid to rest on Monday. Had it not been my dad, we would have laughed at the difunto that rolled around like an alberjon maduro from one place to another.

"May the angel of the Lord come to meet you," sang my cousins as my dad was lowered into the ground.

Contributors

ED CHÁVEZ
has had poetry and short stories published in *Viaztlán, Voces/ Voices,* and *Tierra.* His novel about the Cinco de Mayo, *The Cry of the Gloriana,* was published in 1991. Chávez was born and now lives in Albuquerque with his wife and three children. He works for Social Security.

DAGOBERTO GILB
has worked in construction for sixteen years, much of the time as a union carpenter. His short fiction has appeared regularly over the past decade in publications such as *The Threepenny Review.* More recent publications have been included in two of the *Best of the West* series, as well as other anthologies. A collection of his fiction, *Winners on the Pass Line,* was published in 1985. Born and raised in Los Angeles, he lives in El Paso.

INÉS HERNÁNDEZ
teaches at the University of California, Davis. She has published a collection of poetry entitled *Con razón corazón.*

MARÍA HERRERA-SOBEK'S
publications include: *The Bracero Experience: Elitelore versus Folklore, Beyond Stereotypes: The Critical Analysis of Chicana Literature,* and *The Mexican Corrido: A Feminist Analysis.* She coedited *Chicana Creativity and Criticism: Charting New Frontiers in American Literature* with Helena Viramontes and *Saga de México* with Seymour Menton. She is one of three poets featured in the anthology *Three Times a Woman.* She is a professor at the University of California, Irvine.

JOEL HUERTA
is from Edinburgh, Texas. He has published poems in *Puerto del Sol, Cutbank,* and other journals. He attended Rice University and the University of Arizona. He lives in Austin where he is a doctoral student at the University of Texas.

RITA MAGDALENO
is a Tucson poet who teaches at Pima Community College and develops creative writing workshops. Her work has appeared in *Puerto, Taos Review, Brown Review,* and in several anthologies including *After Aztlán: Latino Poets in the Nineties* and an anthology of Arizona literature, edited by Greg McNamee. She was a featured reader in 1991 at the Bisbee Poetry Festival and the Inter-American Bookfair in San Antonio.

MIGUEL MÉNDEZ
is the author of several creative works including *Peregrinos de Aztlán* (novel), *El sueño de Santa María de las Piedras* (novel), *Los criaderos humanos* (poetry), and *Que no mueran los sueños* (short stories). His novels have been translated into English. In 1990 he was awarded the prestigious José Fuentes Mares Award. He was born in Bisbee, Arizona, and raised in Sonora. He is a professor of literature at the University of Arizona in the Department of Spanish and Portuguese.

ARLENE MESTAS
is a writer living in Española, New Mexico.

PAT MORA
has published three poetry collections: *Chants, Borders,* and *Communion.* Three of her children's books are forthcoming from Macmillan and Knopf. She is completing a book of personal essays in Cincinnati where she now lives.

G. ALEX OLVERA
was born and raised in downtown Los Angeles. He migrated north to the San Francisco Bay area where he earned a B.A. in Creative Writing at the University of California, Santa Cruz. Presently, he teaches sixth grade in the San Fernando Valley in Southern California.

EMILIA PAREDES
was born in the state of Washington of Peruvian immigrant parents. She received a B.A. in psychology from Loma Linda University and her M.S.W. from the University of California, Berkeley. Her poems are based on her stay on the island of Gomera in the Canary Islands. It is the same island from which Columbus sailed on his first voyage to the West Indies.

MARGARITA TAVERA RIVERA
was born in the state of Guanajuato and grew up in the lower Río Grande Valley. She dropped out of the tenth grade, and for the next few years she and her family joined the hundreds of families that followed the migrant stream. She has picked cotton in Texas, potatoes in Idaho, berries in Oregon, and green onions in Arizona. She says, "I hate onions." She holds three M.A. degrees and a doctorate. Her dream is to be able to devote her time to writing full-time.

ROWENA RIVERA
received her Ph.D. from the University of Colorado, and has taught at several Colorado universities and at the University of New Mexico. Inspired by border Spanish and the folk traditions of Southern New Mexico and the El Paso area where she was born, she has written fiction since her high-school years. Her novel, *Las huellas de los sueños*, will soon be published by Grijalbo Press of Mexico City.